D1230531

Praise for *Physician Leadership*

"Leadership in healthcare is not a 'lifetime achievement award,' but is, in truth, the set of learned knowledge and applied skills with which a leader inspires others to achieve what they believe is beyond their reach, and in many cases, to inspire the future leaders of our professions. We are constantly acquiring new knowledge and building new shills. *Physician Leadership* is well organized and thoughtfully annotated and will provide a useful framework to build a practical leadership foundation for those on a lifelong leadership journey, as related by one of the most respected leaders in our field."

—Jeffrey P. Gold, MD, Chancellor, University of Nebraska Medical Center

"I heard Dr. Nichols's voice as I read this—kind and wise. She is an ubermentor and friend to our profession. We need her voice now more than ever."

—Christian T. Cable, MD, MHPE, FACP, FACOI, Director of Graduate Medical Education, Baylor Scott & White Health, Temple, TX

"To call Dr. Nichols a trailblazer would be a gross understatement. In this book, she 'pays it forward' with lessons and advice that will guide the aspiring physician leader on a path to success. I highly recommend this well-referenced work to all such physicians."

—Boyd Buser, DO, FACOFP *dist.*, Past President, American Osteopathic Association Clinical Professor, University of New England College of Osteopathic Medicine

"This personal, provocative, and principled leadership roadmap reveals that although physicians may be smart and educated, under challenging conditions, their knowledge and skills don't necessarily translate to the essentials of leading diverse teams, institutions, and communities."

—Clinton E. Adams, DO, FACHE RDML, MC, USN (RET), President and Chief Executive Officer, Rocky Vista University

"Karen Nichols, D.O., presents a refreshing, practical, realistic, engaging, and personal guide on becoming an effective physician leader. She challenges the assumption that physician clinical expertise is synonymous with, and easily transferable to, 'effective' physician leadership. *Physician Leadership* presents a comparative analysis of physician skills versus leadership skills that is masterful. Dr. Nichols shares her lessons learned in a personalized manner that is relatable for physicians who aspire to lead. A must-read."

—Barbara Ross-Lee, D.O., M.A., FACOFP, President-elect, American Osteopathic Foundation

"Dr. Nichols draws important parallels between the physician's comfort in their role as a physician and discomfort in their role as a leader. This honest and approachable book is critically important for the physician who is struggling to find their voice and to contribute to leadership positions both inside and outside the house of medicine."

—Natasha Bray, DO, MSEd, Associate Dean of Academic Affairs, Clinical Associate Professor, Associate Dean of Accreditation, Oklahoma State University, College of Osteopathic Medicine at the Cherokee Nation

"Are you an excellent physician who wants to take the next step to leadership? Dr. Nichols' book, with its practical, conversational style, will guide you through the steps of knowing your own leadership strengths and areas in need of further growth. *Physician Leadership* will help you develop the skills you will need to succeed."

—Jessica L. Bienstock, MD, MPH Professor, Associate Dean for Graduate Medical Education / Designated Institutional Official, Johns Hopkins University School of Medicine

"In this book, Dr. Nichols shares a step-by-step roadmap guide on how to elevate your leadership skills and become a transformative, visionary, and most importantly, successful leader in healthcare. This practical guide is not only full of incredibly useful and impactful information, but unlike many other leadership books, it is also infused with personality and anecdotes that allow the reader to see the evolution of their leadership development laid out in a very clear roadmap to success. All exceptional physicians are not exceptional leaders, and the tools needed to be a transformative leader are not taught in medical school curriculum. This book fills that need and lays out the groundwork for how to take your career to the next level in a practical and intentional way."

—**Shikha Jain, MD, FACP, Assistant Professor of Medicine, Division of Hematology and Oncology, Director of Communication Strategies in Medicine, University of Illinois Chicago, Associate Director of Oncology Communication & Digital Innovation, University of Illinois Cancer Center Chief Operating Officer, Co-Founder, IMPACT, Chair, Co-Founder, Women In Medicine Summit**

"Never has there been a more important time for leadership in healthcare. Many of us have learned to lead in medicine through the mentorship of our peers and by dedicating our lives to advocating for our colleagues, trainees, patients, and profession. In *Physician Leadership,* Dr. Nichols provides an excellent compilation of well-researched tools and shares her experience from a lifetime of leadership to allow young leaders to shorten their journeys toward success."

—**Robert S. Juhasz, DO, MACOI, FACP, 118th President of the American Osteopathic Association, Clinical Professor of Medicine, OU Heritage College of Osteopathic Medicine, Contributing Author of *New Horizons in Patient Safety: Understanding Communication: Case Studies for Physicians***

"Karen Nichols, D.O. is a 'leader's leader' and a 'teacher's teacher.' Her acumen and basic, well founded approach to leadership skills are not only based on years of multidisciplinary clinical and administrative leadership, but her true sense of the basics of complementary collaboration. She is able to compile the concepts of 'leadership training' into a common sense treatise on nonclinical 'physician leadership.' Her format and presentation make this instructional book a true treasure to read, re-read, and practice."

—**Thomas Ely, D.O., FAAFP, FACOFP, FAAOE, President, American Osteopathic Association LTC (Ret.) US Army**

"In this book, which provides a roadmap for physician leadership, the gifted Dr. Karen Nichols brilliantly compares and contrasts the skills that we attain during our training as doctors with the skill set needed for good leadership. She masterfully discusses one's personal approach to leadership, communication skills, perspective, decision-making, character, emotional intelligence, negotiation skills, conflict management, the art of persuasion, managing change, and meeting dynamics with just the right amount of humor and poignant examples with workbook style questions when appropriate. I especially enjoyed the nod to osteopathic medicine. This book is very well referenced and is a 'must-read' for leaders in medicine, both old and new."

—Roberta E. Gebhard, D.O., 2019-2020 President of the American Medical Women's Association American Medical Association Women Physician Section Governing Council Member, TIME'S UP Healthcare Advisory Board Member, Physicians Just Equity Advisory Board Member

"Here's the book we've been waiting for. All the steps needed to take you from being a great physician to a great physician leader, from a true expert in the field. Dr. Nichols has created a roadmap to success that is worth your read."

—Margaret A. Wilson, D.O., Chair AACOM Board of Deans, Dean, Professor Department of Family Medicine, Kirksville College of Osteopathic Medicine, A.T. Still University

"It will be a great leader resource."

—Richard S. Dobrusin, D.O., MS(Ost) FACOFP, President, Arizona Osteopathic Medical Association

"Dr. Nichols, your book is WONDERFUL! Wow! The lessons and insight you provide readers is INVALUABLE, and you do this in a personal and practical way. The examples you use in the book are personal and relatable, and the style in which you deliver information is clear and usable. Readers will gain so much from your knowledge and experiences through this step-by-step manual on how to be an effective physician-leader! Brava!"

—Dr. Jen Caudle, Family Physician, Associate Professor, Rowan University

"Dr. Nichols's roadmap is essential reading for physician leaders. Readers will learn the 11 essential topics through anecdotes and reflective prompts, providing a practical guide *specifically* for physicians. Physicians are well-trained to approach diagnostic mysteries in a systematic way, but those skills are not readily translatable to leadership of teams or organizations. Through Dr. Nichols's *Physician Leadership,* physicians charged with leadership roles can learn the 11 essential topics to become a successful physician leader. The book takes a deep dive into each essential topic through personal anecdotes and provides a practical guide to application of these topics through reflective questions. Leaders at every stage will find sage advice and guidance on navigating the challenges surrounding the transition from astute clinician to physician leader.

As a junior faculty member trying to navigate the waters of leadership in organized medicine, I found Dr. Nichols's *Physician Leadership* to contain a wealth of practical advice and concepts readily applicable to the unforeseen challenges I've faced as a physician leader. It's a resource I anticipate returning to time and time again."

—Amanda S. Xi, MD, Critical Care Anesthesiologist, Massachusetts General Hospital/Harvard Medical School

"I have enjoyed reading your manuscript from front to back."

—Edith P. Mitchell, MD, MACP, FCPP, FRCP, Clinical Professor of Medicine and Medical Oncology, Department of Medical Oncology, Director, Center to Eliminate Cancer Disparities, Associate Director, Diversity Affairs, Sidney Kimmel Cancer Center at Jefferson, 116th President National Medical Association

"I have had the privilege of observing and working with Dr. Nichols for many years as she ascended through the ranks of the organizations of the osteopathic profession. She has excelled at each level – from osteopathic student, resident, fellow, and AOA Board member to the office of president of the American Osteopathic Association. She has set the bar high for all that have had the privilege of working and serving with her. I count myself as part of those that have had the privilege of knowing and working with her.

Dr. Nichols proved herself to not only to be a superior student but also a superior practicing physician. She established a reputation as a very-well-prepared physician as she demonstrated her caring, compassion, and skills as a practicing physician. Her practice, skills, and knowledge were sought by other physicians in practice and future physicians as students and residents.

Moreover, her leadership skills were recognized by other physicians in training, in osteopathic organizations, and ultimately AOA board members from state and specialty colleges. These recognitions were evident as she was supported by all to be promoted to the high office of president of the American Osteopathic Association. There is no better evidence of the high esteem for Dr. Nichols held by many in the osteopathic profession who supported her to be the leader of our osteopathic profession as our president . . . the first of her gender to be so recognized."
        —William G. Anderson, D.O. FACOS, AOA Past President

"Karen Nichols has never regarded past precedents as an obstacle to future achievements. I first met Karen when I started practicing medicine in Mesa, Arizona, in 1991. She was the first female chief of staff of Mesa General Hospital. It was obvious to me even then that she was born to lead, teach, and inspire. I remember going to the hospital one day and having the opportunity to watch how Karen interacted with a family during a stressful situation. I observed her demeanor and her ability to be present with this family in this difficult time. Her level of competence, compassion, and empathy was the highest I had ever seen. It was one of the greatest learning experiences of my medical career, and I committed to trying to emulate this type of behavior in my own actions. Everyone who worked at the hospital back then knew that she was headed for greatness.

The list of firsts in Karen's accomplishments is endless. She was the first recipient of the physician of the year award from The Arizona Osteopathic Medical Association (AOMA). She also received the AOMA lifetime achievement award. She served as the first female president of the AOMA, the American College of Osteopathic Internists (ACOI), and the American Osteopathic Association (AOA). She is the first osteopathic chair of the board of the Accreditation Council for Graduate Medical Education. She received the AOA's highest honor, the Presidential Citation. She served as the dean of the Chicago College of Osteopathic Medicine. She was prominently featured in the documentary and book *The Feminine Touch: Women in Osteopathic Medicine*. It would be considerably easier to list the awards and accomplishments that Karen has not received rather than those she has. Karen has also shined as a nationally recognized speaker. Her presentations are captivating, entertaining, and informative on multiple topics.

Karen's commitment to and passion for osteopathic medicine and the profession has never wavered. She has inspired countless women (and men) to follow in her footsteps. She is smart, kind, and incredibly talented in all her endeavors. She has a gift of making the person with whom she is speaking to feel like they are the center of her attention.

Theodore Roosevelt has said that 'People don't care what you know until they know that you care.' Karen interacts with poise and dignity, and it is obvious that she cares. I so look forward to more wisdom from her in this book, and in the coming years.

—Richard S. Dobrusin, D.O., FACOFP,
President Arizona Osteopathic Medical Association

PHYSICIAN
LEADERSHIP

Karen J. Nichols, DO

PHYSICIAN
LEADERSHIP

The 11 Skills
Every Doctor Needs
to be an Effective
Leader

WILEY

Copyright © 2021 by John Wiley & Sons, Inc. All rights reserved.

Published by John Wiley & Sons, Inc., Hoboken, New Jersey.
Published simultaneously in Canada.

No part of this publication may be reproduced, stored in a retrieval system, or transmitted in any form
or by any means, electronic, mechanical, photocopying, recording, scanning, or otherwise, except as
permitted under Section 107 or 108 of the 1976 United States Copyright Act, without either the
prior written permission of the Publisher, or authorization through payment of the appropriate per-
copy fee to the Copyright Clearance Center, Inc., 222 Rosewood Drive, Danvers, MA 01923, (978)
750-8400, fax (978) 646-8600, or on the Web at www.copyright.com. Requests to the Publisher for
permission should be addressed to the Permissions Department, John Wiley & Sons, Inc., 111 River
Street, Hoboken, NJ 07030, (201) 748-6011, fax (201) 748-6008, or online at http://www.wiley.com/
go/permissions.

Limit of Liability/Disclaimer of Warranty: While the publisher and author have used their best efforts
in preparing this book, they make no representations or warranties with respect to the accuracy
or completeness of the contents of this book and specifically disclaim any implied warranties of
merchantability or fitness for a particular purpose. No warranty may be created or extended by sales
representatives or written sales materials. The advice and strategies contained herein may not be
suitable for your situation. You should consult with a professional where appropriate. Neither the
publisher nor author shall be liable for any loss of profit or any other commercial damages, including
but not limited to special, incidental, consequential, or other damages.

For general information on our other products and services or for technical support, please contact
our Customer Care Department within the United States at (800) 762-2974, outside the United
States at (317) 572-3993 or fax (317) 572-4002.

Wiley publishes in a variety of print and electronic formats and by print-on-demand. Some material
included with standard print versions of this book may not be included in e-books or in print-on-
demand. If this book refers to media such as a CD or DVD that is not included in the version you
purchased, you may download this material at http://booksupport.wiley.com. For more information
about Wiley products, visit www.wiley.com.

Library of Congress Cataloging-in-Publication Data

Names: Nichols, Karen J., author.
Title: Physician leadership : the 11 skills every doctor needs to be an
   effective leader / Karen J. Nichols, DO, MA, MACOI, FACP, CS-F.
Description: Hoboken, New Jersey : Wiley, [2021] | Includes index.
Identifiers: LCCN 2021034682 (print) | LCCN 2021034683 (ebook) | ISBN
   9781119817543 (Hardcover) | ISBN 9781119817574 (ePDF) | ISBN
   9781119817550 (ePub)
Subjects: LCSH: Leadership. | Physicians. | Health services administration.
   | Organizational effectiveness.
Classification: LCC HD57.7 .N53 2021 (print) | LCC HD57.7 (ebook) | DDC
   362.17/2068—dc23
LC record available at https://lccn.loc.gov/2021034682
LC ebook record available at https://lccn.loc.gov/2021034683

COVER DESIGN: PAUL MCCARTHY
COVER ART: © GETTY IMAGES | NORA CAROL PHOTOGRAPHY
SKY10028252_072021

This book is dedicated to my husband, Jim Nichols. I could never have accomplished any of the things I have in life without his unwavering commitment and support. He always puts my needs and goals ahead of his own and often does so without me even knowing. Because of him, I was able to become a physician, an internist, and a leader. He is truly the "wind beneath my wings." I owe everything to him, and I dedicate this book to him.

"Two roads diverged in a wood, and I –
I took the one less traveled by,
And that has made all the difference."

—Robert Frost

Contents

Contents

Foreword

This might be the first book you will read about leadership, but if you are like me, a collection of books about leadership sits on one or more shelves somewhere in your home. The number of titles has likely increased over the years. The path to becoming a better leader is somewhat like finding the Templar Treasure in the movie *National Treasure*. There is always another clue—another book offering pearls of wisdom. I have my favorite authors, like John Maxwell and John Kotter, who've provided me with clues along the path.

One type of clue to better leadership has been missing. Until reading I hadn't actually thought about the absence of a book about leadership written for physicians by a physician. I have only one that comes close, *Designed to Adapt* by John Kenagy, MD. It isn't specifically a guide to prepare physicians for leadership roles but does offer the reader an opportunity to improve their leadership skills while outlining a model for improving our health care system.

Within the pages of my book collection and stuffed into other note-books and files are my favorite go-to leadership tools—part of the quest for the leadership treasure. I pull them out and use them when I'm experiencing a specific problem. The challenge with having too many tools in too many locations is the passage of time. It is easy to forget them if unused. In which book was that 2 × 2 table about decision-making? It's always fun to discover them again and wish you hadn't forgotten about them in the first place.

I don't think I'm going to forget about this book. Why is that? The first is the author. Dr. Karen Nichols is an amazing individual. For me and many others, she is a combination of colleague, friend, mentor, and coach. She seems to possess boundless energy and always has time to listen and help others. Her sense of purpose never seems to waver, and her impact on others continues to grow, mostly because she lives leadership—exactly as described in her book.

The true leader is constantly growing—a lifelong learner trying to improve how they help and motivate others to do things they might not otherwise do. One might think we don't need another book about leadership, particularly a book describing yet another new leadership model. Most of us just need to get better at the basics. That is exactly what makes different.

It is written *for* physicians *by* a physician—providing very practical information on how to become a leader or how to become a better leader. I think the topic found its author in this work—an author who embodies the best of leadership in daily life. The construct is essentially a how-to guide, filled with a summary of the best and most useful tools from other recognized works and original materials from the author applied to challenging situations that physician leaders will face. Along the way, the author weaves in the story of her remarkable life. She is passionate about osteopathic medicine and promoting women in leadership.

Its collective chapters remind me of one of those multipurpose tools that can help you out in many situations. You just have to know how each tool works and practice using them. For me, it may no longer be necessary to search through my books, files, and notebooks to look for a long-lost clue. Dr. Nichols has assembled many of them in one location.

Karen has been writing this book her whole life. I learned (and remembered) a lot by reading it, and I am sure you will as well! You can't master it all, but a person wanting to be a stronger leader can keep trying. Perhaps derived from this work there is a great course ahead! I know that I would attend.

Robert A. Cain, DO
March 2021

Introduction:
Best Practice in
Medicine and
Leadership Are Not
Always the Same

You have been in practice a few years and you are invited to serve on a committee, in the hospital or in the practice group or in a health system. You serve with distinction, and you are asked to chair the next committee that is formed.

"Finally!" you think, "My talents and leadership skills have been recognized!"

But something goes wrong.

The committee doesn't listen to what you say. The committee wants to do something different than what is very clearly the right direction. The committee even questions your leadership! What is wrong with them? The committee achieves a semblance of the goal, and yet it's not the best it could be. Lesson learned. Get better committee members the next time.

The next time comes. You are again appointed to head up a committee. This time, you are more careful about whom you select for committee members. Of course, you don't get to select all the committee members, and now you know which people share a similar view of the situation and its focus.

It doesn't go well again! They don't LISTEN!! The people who had a similar view of the situation got swayed by those who didn't. What's that old joke? It's a zombie solution – it works, but badly. Another missed opportunity.

THIS time you're ready for the next new committee. You push to get all the best people appointed to the committee. They agree with your view; they will follow what you say, and you can get this moved through quickly.

They followed your lead, implemented your plan, pretty much, and guess what? Another zombie solution! You were the leader – you are a respected doctor, after all! What is wrong with these people??

You decide it is time to talk to your very kind and wise mentor.

"I don't get it! I know what I'm doing. I understand the situation. I explain it clearly, and it's still not working! I don't know how to get better committee members so we can get better work done!"

The mentor takes a moment for a deep breath. Then she says those fateful words:

"Maybe the problem isn't getting better committee members. Maybe the committee needs a better leader."

Ouch!!

"I don't have time to read a lot of books or listen to podcasts. I don't have time to do a five-day leadership conference! I am a very busy doctor, for heaven's sakes! My patients need me! Besides, I'm smart enough to figure out anything. In fact, that is what I do all day, every day!"

You begin to wonder if maybe that mentor is not quite so kind as you thought, when she says. . .

"You've tried leading three times already, so it would appear that if you could have figured it out, you would have done so by now."

Double ouch!

Hence, this little book. This doctor is me. Unfortunately, I didn't go to a kind and wise mentor to get this good advice after just three tries at leadership. I've been a leader all my life. My three younger sisters still call me "bossy." After one "instruction" session in the backyard, one of my sisters said, "You are not the boss of me!"

But I always assumed that I was! The evidence started early. In the Christmas pageant, I was one of the group of 4-year-olds who had been taught to sing a song as we marched around the entire 15-feet oval area down front in the church where the pulpit was positioned. However, as each succeeding child followed the one ahead, they effectively cut off the end of the oval, in order to follow more closely the one ahead. By the time I was the next in line to walk around the oval, it was not an oval anymore, it was more like a 3-feet circle. This would never do. I knew what we were expected to do and led the rest of the group of 4-year-olds all the way around the full oval. That generated no end of comments from the parents. I was just leading!

Clearly, those "guidance opportunities" provided early leadership training. I was president of every organization in which I participated before matriculating at Kansas City College of Osteopathic Medicine (KCCOM) (now KCU-COM): vice president of my class four times at KCCOM; chief resident at the 500 bed Oklahoma Osteopathic Hospital; president of the Arizona Osteopathic Medical Association, the American College of Osteopathic Internists, and the American Osteopathic Association. It has always been very clear to me that I am a doctor, and all doctors are leaders, right? Remember, I'm an internist, and as the old line goes, "Maybe wrong, but never in doubt!"

I'm the one who wished I had had this little roadmap. It took years of reading, conferences, practice, and trial and error to learn these lessons. And I had a master's degree in Management with a specialty in health care administration before I went to DO school! *It is a painfully true statement that I have made every mistake in the book!* Sam Levinson said, "You must learn from the mistakes of others, it takes too long to make all those mistakes yourself." In retrospect, it would appear I have tried to make all the mistakes, believe me – just not on purpose. Another helpful perspective that I tell myself is that there are no mistakes, only lessons, and lessons don't work if you don't put them into practice.

There is also a painful truth about physicians. Physicians are smart. Physicians are educated and trained in one of the most challenging topics known to man: the care and maintenance of human beings. So, when we physicians are launched into patient care in an unsupervised practice capacity, we are ready to go! We are also set up to fall into a huge trap in the rest of life's activities. Completing the arduous process to be educated and trained in medicine naturally results in developing an appropriate degree of confidence in the knowledge, skills, and abilities to be a physician. Unfortunately, that knowledge and those skills don't translate into mastery of other topics; witness investment mistakes, misbegotten land purchase deals, failed joint partnerships, you name it, which brings us back to: leadership. Physician knowledge and skills are not inherently fungible or scalable to other topics, despite the self-perceived assumptions and confidence to the contrary.

Thus, these are the 11 things you must have nailed down to move to the next level of developing knowledge and skills. This book is a roadmap. Master these points and move to the next level. The problem I have frequently seen is that the physician who wishes to lead leaps into learning finance and wage and salary administration. All worthy and important topics. However, when she doesn't understand principles of communication, persuasion, and conflict management, as examples, she can't effectively implement those next-level skills.

There are some important differences between being a great physician and being a great physician leader. I cannot emphasize enough that some approaches and skills that we are taught as being emblematic of the best approach a physician can employ do actually work well when transferred to the leadership sphere. The big stumbling block we physicians run into is when the medical care paradigm we employ is not the appropriate leadership approach and may actually be the opposite and contraindicated.

Here is the expected response from our new physician leader, both here and throughout this book, with her comments italicized to identify our conversations. And her first response:

"Seriously? I'm a terrific physician. Well regarded and well respected for my clinical skill, acumen, and approach. How can that be bad?"

Stay tuned. We will cover what works and what doesn't.

A further caution comes from Stanford's Jeffrey Pfeffer (Fox 2006): Good leaders can make a small positive difference; bad leaders can make a huge negative difference. Yikes!

Chapter Overview

So, I have set up this roadmap for physicians like me to get the basic principles behind what makes leadership work. This book covers the essence of leadership in the form of brief summaries of 11 topics. We will cover the following:

Chapter 1 – How to discover and understand your *personal approach and style* to thinking and interactions, as well as that of others, and how that information can and will move your agenda forward more effectively.

Physician Approach

I don't know many physicians who know there are different personal approaches, let alone what theirs might be and how that impacts their interactions. In my practice of internal medicine, I never had any idea. I'm the doctor. I tell it like it is. What is wrong with that? There may not be anything wrong with that approach as a physician.

Leader Approach

This chapter will guide you in getting to a much more effective understanding of your approach and that of others and why, as a leader, understanding your approach and that of others can make or break your leadership efficacy. Simple as that.

Chapter 2 – How to employ *principles of communication* to accomplish your objectives.

Physician Approach

Communicate?? I can talk to my patients, I can translate their medical situation into lay language, I can answer their questions. I have learned that over the years and have honed my skills. OK, good, that approach works well for the physician.

Leader Approach
In the leadership realm, just telling someone what is happening and what
to do about it is often one of the least effective ways to lead. There is a
lot more to communication than just telling people what to do.

Chapter 3 – How to implement *practical techniques of communication* to
good effect.

Physician Approach
These points go into new territory far beyond what we usually must
employ with our patients.

Leader Approach
In the same vein as in Chapter 2, there are proven techniques of communication to accomplish the goals of the leader. Follow this roadmap!

Chapter 4 – How *perspectives,* yours and others, impact and are impacted
by the organization's culture and how those perspectives affect your leadership effectiveness.

Physician Approach
Physicians have to consider different perspectives when working with
patients who come from other socio-economic and educational backgrounds, cultures, age groups, genders, and ethnicities.

Leader Approach
As a leader, this consideration of perspectives is crucial and very similar to
what a physician needs to do.

Chapter 5 – What are effective approaches to *decision-making* to get to
better solutions with better buy-in? How can unintended consequences
lead any decision-making process off the rails?

Physician Approach
Physicians are usually good decision makers for and with their patients, if
they understand what the patient hears and wants. And one of the reasons we are so good at this is because we have been trained thoroughly

to know the options, questions, and implications that are available. Research has shown that the physician leader steps through the entire decision tree about a medical issue (for example, steps A–J to reach conclusion/decision K). And having done that so many times, it may look like the physician made a snap decision, skipping several levels of consideration, but that is not what happened. After a time, even the physician may not have realized they automatically went through all those steps, but they did. This is commonly known as creating and evaluating a differential diagnosis, something doctors do very well.

Leader Approach
The challenge for physician leaders is that we haven't been trained in any of these points/steps about leadership considerations. So, in a leadership situation with the same number of critical steps in the decision tree as above, the physician may jump from A directly to K. However, they didn't have the same education/preparation to learn about all the intermediate steps, as they did in a medical setting, in order to accurately reach an appropriate conclusion/decision. Physician leaders often don't even think about creating a differential diagnosis in a leadership situation. Very dangerous road conditions ahead!

Chapter 6 – This chapter is about *decision-making that doesn't work, and why not.*

Physician Approach
This is not a big topic of concern for physicians. Medical decision-making is part of the medical approach.

Leader Approach
However, as a physician leader, understanding the kinds of issues that sabotage what looked like a good decision is crucial. This is a critical chapter for physician leaders to learn from, as it deals with challenges the physician seldom if ever has to even think about. This is another area where this roadmap guides the novice physician leader through as-yet untraveled territory.

Chapter 7 – How your *character* guides your personal approach, which affects your *interpersonal relationships.*

Physician and Leader Approach

Here is a point where there is complete alignment between being a physician and a leader. There is only one standard for character. Honorable and ethical, every day in every way.

Chapter 8 – How your *relationships,* enhanced by employing emotional intelligence, can make or break your leadership. Further, developing good relationships becomes the backbone of *building teams.*

Physician Approach

As a physician, we may be in a "captain of the ship" position. Emotional intelligence can be employed to create a more conducive environment to better understand our patients, but often it may not be necessary. However, in the setting of hospitals and health care systems with the need for building teams and promoting inter-professional collaboration, relationship-building is becoming a greater part of the practice of medicine.

Leader Approach

As a physician leader, either understanding or ignoring the importance of relationships and how to build and nurture them will literally make or break you. Road map, here we come!

Chapter 9 – What are the basic steps to employ effective *negotiation skills?*

Physician Approach

I challenge any physician to embrace the fact that they must negotiate to get what their patient needs. We are physicians – we *know* what our patients need! The need to negotiate implies that I will be trading things my patients need in order to get approval for things my patients need even more! This cannot be the way medicine should be practiced. Physicians should advocate for what is best for their patients, not negotiate and accept a lesser option.

Leader Approach

However, as a leader, such negotiating skills are critical. The well-intentioned physician leader who demands what is "right" and refuses to negotiate will lose every time; another roadmap thing.

Chapter 10 – What are the *principles of conflict management?*

Physician Approach

Conflict management for the physician is very different from conflict management as a leader. What is the most common conflict that physicians must manage? Getting approval for the appropriate treatment/ drug/surgery. We are well trained and have this information at our fingertips for our patients' medical issues.

Leader Approach

Conflict management as a leader is a very different animal. Once again, the physician is trained in all aspects of the medical issues of a particular presentation. However, in a leadership role, the conflicts arise because of different perspectives, experiences, backgrounds, a whole host of issues. And physicians are not accorded deference in a leadership situation just because they are physicians. Boy, is that annoying!!

Chapter 11 – What are the *tenets of persuasion,* and how do they have a big influence on what you and others decide to do, most of which you are not even aware of?

Physician Approach

Physicians sometimes do have to persuade patients to select a course of action that the physician knows will get them to their stated goal. The wise physician will consider the background of the patient, previous experiences of the patient and their family, and misperceptions perpetuated by the internet or friends and family, for example. However, this occurs at a very basic level. And the persuasiveness is enhanced by the authority of the physician (one of the principles of persuasion that works to our benefit).

Leader Approach

The physician leader must have a thorough understanding of principles of persuasion and which ones will be most effective in leading to the desired outcome. The science of persuasion has been heavily studied, and the physician leader must understand which principles fit which situation and can be employed to move the group in the most successful direction. Skip this chapter at your peril! Hazardous road conditions ahead!

Chapter 12 – How to *manage change* to promote successful leadership.

Physician Approach

Understanding change comes naturally to the physician. The newest drug, the newest surgical technique all change all the time, sometimes at breakneck speed. The physician must and does adapt.

Leader Approach

As a physician leader, it is less clear how change alters the leadership picture. It certainly does; the challenge is the physician can't easily learn about the changes from the latest medical journal because those changes occur in the legal system, the mergers/acquisitions that fly by, the governmental interventions, the insurance companies, the health systems and on and on. An unforeseen/ignored change in any one of these components of the health care delivery system can severely disrupt your leadership. The physician leader who doesn't understand how to successfully implement change is severely handicapped as a leader. The medical and political climate speaks to the importance of this emphasis.

Chapter 13 – What are specific *meeting dynamics* that can aid or sabotage your purpose?

Physician Approach

In the care of patients, there are not a lot of meetings that directly impact the care of a specific patient, other than a tumor board, which is carefully scripted and conducted in a very traditional way.

Leader Approach

The physician leader who doesn't understand the impact of meeting dynamics on effective leadership is seldom going to be able to achieve their desired goals. And will never figure out why. Thus this roadmap!

Chapter 14 – How the physician leader functions as a *whole person*. This is a perspective chapter addressing issues that both women and men physicians and physician leaders must wrestle with. And this focus covers all the issues now seen in diversity, equity, and inclusion.

Chapter 15 – Summarize the *big picture*.

Yes, the big picture summarized in this chapter is a strictly leadership thing, as the big picture for the physician is the patient. And that is as it should be.

"I thought you said there were 11 topics. How did we get to 15 chapters?"

Good question. Some topics are dealt with in two chapters. You will get the basic concept in one chapter and the practical techniques in the second chapter. And there is a bonus chapter dealing with issues of being a whole person as a physician, especially as a physician who is a woman, one of the minority groups in medicine, and who is coming from a specialty, internal medicine, that has been underrepresented in many organizations in which I have participated. Its not exactly a topic with defined principles and techniques in the same way as the other 11 topics, but it has pertinent and important perspectives for physician leaders from many diverse groups.

This roadmap summarizes the topic and then provides the connections to the tried-and-true resource documents when you get stuck or are ready to dive into the details. Each chapter will present the idea in a basic outline and finish with some questions to guide your understanding of the main points. Each section will also finish with that list of top-notch resources when you are ready to do the deep dive into the topic.

You don't have to read this book in the order presented. You may be fully experienced on some of these topics. You may just need some specific pointers on one topic or another and can go directly there. My caution is that everyone must touch base with Chapters 1 (know yourself) and 2 and 3 (communications) to be sure you have those points nailed down, as everything else builds on them. I do have to add that even if you think you are very familiar with a particular "stretch of this roadmap," you may find that you know the topic as a physician but don't have a full appreciation for the topic as a physician leader.

A caution: Reading articles and books (even this one) will give you ideas, but they can't teach you how to think. The "Five Steps" and the "Three 'Ps'" and every other generic framework for problem-solving are heuristics/rules of thumb. They can describe approaches, but they cannot make you think. Just as in medicine, articles and books are not the gospel; they are just the author pinned down.

Resources

Fox, J. (2006). Secrets of greatness. *Fortune*, October 20, 2006. https://archive
    .fortune.com/magazines/fortune/fortune_archive/2006/10/30/
    8391732/index.htm.

Chapter ONE

Know Yourself! Why Does That Matter?

"Wait a minute! I thought we were going to learn about leadership! This chapter is about knowing yourself. What does that have to do with leadership?"

Yes, we are going to learn about physician leadership, AND you cannot be a leader if you do not know yourself. This is one of the most important points in the leadership journey.

"But I DO know myself, it's just those other people who don't make sense."

I must admit I came to this topic with the same opinion as our novice leader. However, the truth was I did not really know very much about myself or how and why I looked at things the way I do. Let alone that there might be logical, well-documented explanations for why others might look at the same things and see them differently than I do. Who knew? Certainly not me!

The further unspoken implication here is I am right and they are wrong. As a doctor, I didn't have any problem making that assumption.

Let me explain how I came face to face with the impact of different personality types and approaches. When I first became the dean of Midwestern University/Chicago College of Osteopathic Medicine (MWU/CCOM), I knew I had a lot to learn. I did not get my degree from this college of osteopathic medicine (COM); I only knew one or two faculty at the COM and only knew them from medical meetings. I also had never been a dean and I had never worked full time at a COM, so even though I thought I knew what I was supposed to be doing, I was certainly aware that I might be VERY wrong.

I still remember sitting at my desk in my new dean's office about 10 a.m. on my first day, having looked through the two file drawers of papers left by my predecessor and thinking, "So now what do I do?" The idea of a "listening tour" was popular then, so I decided to try that approach. I asked my staff to book an hour appointment with each of the 15 department chairs. I laid out three or four questions to ask each one. They covered the usual concerns for anyone new in a supervisory capacity: What are the biggest issues facing your department and the COM? What should a new dean focus on first? I was ready!

Note: I later discovered *The First 90 Days: Proven Strategies for Getting Up to Speed Faster and Smarter* by Michael Watkins (2013), an excellent guide for conducting this same type of listening tour approach. It is well worth a look when tackling a new position.

What I learned from this listening tour certainly surprised me, but not for the reasons I expected. The answers were enlightening, helpful, and insightful. What I was not prepared for were the different styles and approaches of these people. I am going to describe each response and the type of interaction in the way I encountered these people and their approaches. Over time, I learned about personality classification systems and could go back and see that approach in each of these individuals. Suffice it to say, I just didn't get it at first. Stick with me and we'll circle back to examine each approach. Lest anyone try to identify each chair, I have combined some characteristics and comments to make the approach distinction more clear.

The first chair came in with a thick document of notes outlining the recent history of the COM, what worked, what did not, advice for the future, and cautions regarding other chairs. I never even got a chance to ask my questions, as the entire time was filled with the narrative provided. Talk about "outgoing"!

The next chair sat quietly while I introduced myself. As I asked each question, there was clearly significant thought going into preparing the answers. There were silence gaps in the conversation as I asked my question and the chair quietly sat there and considered the answer before speaking. The answers were well crafted and helpful. I also quickly learned that if I did not ask about a specific point, I didn't get spontaneous input regarding that point, or any others I hadn't thought to ask. So, I had to carefully explore the answers with follow-up questions to be sure I got the full picture. A very quiet thoughtful person.

Statistics were the focus for the next chair. He had every spreadsheet, every data point, and every numerical detail of the topics of concern he wanted to discuss. He knew every board score for every discipline for every year, the annual average GPA by class, the trend for course and board pass rates, the match/placement percentage, every bit of numerical data that could be gleaned from the operation of the COM. A true numbers person.

The next chair started out with a story to illustrate the culture of this COM. He continued to regale me with stories about students, faculty, administrations, and especially about past deans! He knew which deans worked on campus on weekends and which ones left campus the minute the president's car drove away. I didn't get a chance to ask questions, as his stories went on and on. He certainly lived in narratives.

Another chair took a different tack. When I asked about the most difficult challenges facing the COM, he never got to the end of that answer. "X is an issue, Y is an issue, Z is an issue, but actually A, B, and C also cause a lot of challenges." He kept comparing and contrasting a variety of possible answers until our time ran out. Sheesh!

A different approach from another chair appeared to me to be focused on the tortoise tactic for COM management: slow and steady wins the race. Stay the course! The COM is doing well; the COM has lots of applicants, the COM has a great reputation. Why change?

As I worked my way through the meetings with all the chairs, I was struck by how differently each one presented themselves and how differently they answered my questions, assuming I got the chance to ask my questions. Not only did I quickly realize that my concerns about having a lot to learn about the COM were accurate, I also came to appreciate that I had as much if not more to learn about how to work with these chairs.

Most had been at the COM for many years and in the chair role for quite some time, too. The COM had a stellar reputation to be sure, and all the chairs were dedicated to maintaining the excellence of the COM, so I didn't see any need to make immediate and drastic changes. And yet, they were so different from each other. How was I going to figure out how to work with them? Where to start? Now that I had a better understanding of the challenges, the question was how to proceed.

The further problem was that I didn't truly appreciate the variation of the approaches of these chairs, why they took the approaches they did, and what I should do to use those differences to the best advantage for the COM. My initial reaction was that I heard what they said, I understood their points, and I thought the fairest thing was to treat them all the same. Who could disagree with being uniform? Frankly, I was annoyed by the ones who had a different approach than the one I was used to or desired. But I was the dean! They would have to learn how to deal with me! How wrong I was!!

What I had to learn was, there is more to leadership than telling people what to do. Not only were there different personality and approach types, but I needed to learn what those types were, what did those different types bring to the table, and so on. And while I thought I knew my own style, that wasn't true, either. As a doctor in practice for 17 years, I really had never had to consider that there were different approaches. I had just decided what to do in my private practice and did it. It slowly began to occur to me that maybe I had been missing an important piece of why I had such difficulty in getting my hospital and organization committees to work efficiently. Maybe the other committee members were coming with as many different approaches as the new dean (me) found in her chairs. Who knew? Obviously, I had to learn something about personality types and approaches. Where was the roadmap when I needed it?

OK, let's be a little introspective here and start with the dean. The recommendation to "know yourself" is nothing new. The statement "The unexamined life is not worth living" is attributed to Socrates (Plato 399 BCE). I must admit that when I read that statement years ago, I did not really understand it. I interpreted that the admonition was to recommend that I engage in what is known as "navel gazing," or considering who I am and what I am doing. The accurate and more helpful implication goes much further into understanding the basis for our multifaceted personalities.

Further, the importance of this topic has a long presence in the literature. This passage from *Tao Te Ching,* Chapter 33 by Lao-Tzu called "The Taoist Classic" has been variously translated; this translation (Lao-Tzu 2000) is my favorite.

> Knowing others is intelligence.
> Knowing yourself is true wisdom.
> Mastering others requires strength.
> Mastering yourself requires true power.

I also like this statement by Warren Bennis: "Becoming a leader is synonymous with becoming yourself. It is that simple. It is that difficult" (Bennis 2009, xxxvii). In my opinion, his statement is spot on, because "becoming yourself" has to be preceded by "knowing yourself." Truly understanding yourself is difficult and very important. If you know how you approach and how you react to situations, it is easier to be comfortable with that reality so you can accept and become who you are.

"Ok! I get it! I'll give it a shot. Let's get started!"

There are several instruments to assess personality approaches and are referenced in the following resource section. The most longstanding and highly utilized personality assessment instrument is the Myers-Briggs Type Indicator (MBTI). The basic idea is that there are four personality characteristics that have dichotomous options. I/E (introvert/extrovert), N/S (intuitive/sensing), T/F (thinking/feeling), and J/P (judging/perceiving) (Myers-Briggs and Myers 1980; Myers-Briggs 1993). With four different letters in each of the dichotomous choices, there are 16 combinations. The most predictive of behavior is the middle pair. Therefore, most analysts look at the middle pair of letters together. There are abbreviated versions of the MBTI survey instrument online so you can get a taste of the concept. However, if you want to dive in, it is most helpful to get the full MBTI picture with the purchased and professionally assessed version, as each person's categorization of the four characteristics will fall along a continuum. For example, while I categorize as an extrovert, I am fairly close on the continuum to crossing the line that would then classify me as an introvert.

Please note that some will point out that the MBTI developed organically and was not based on our usual research protocols. I would agree that it is not wise to be slavishly dedicated to MBTI or any other rubric as a rigid and immutable classification. That does not diminish the point that people bring different approaches to discussions, issues, and problems, which need to be acknowledged and appreciated.

"OK, now I know my full type, but I don't know what type other people might be. How do I figure that out? It's not likely that everyone has done these assessments, and wouldn't it be prying to ask everyone what type they are anyway?"

Yes, so let's look back at the chairs I introduced earlier. The first chair bowled me over with intensity and eagerness to talk. Not being impolite, just being more of an (E) extrovert. The next chair seemed almost uninterested in the discussion, speaking only when spoken to and not volunteering unasked but applicable information. He was not disinterested or lacking in ideas, just demonstrating more of an introvert (I) approach.

Then came along the statistics-focused chair (most likely ST) and then the stories/people-focused (most likely NF) chair. Here were two very different emphases selected from the exact same shared experiences.

How about that chair who never seemed to settle on a final determination of what were the most significant issues for the COM? I have come to learn that is much more of a "P-perceiving" approach as opposed to a "J-judging" approach in the MBTI spectrum. As a strong J, I was always frustrated by the person who could not seem to pick an answer. After studying more about personality approaches, I came to see that the strong P was doing a more thorough job of bringing up some additional viable options in a situation, even better than I did.

So the most important thing is to know that there are other types, and when one approach employed by you isn't working, it is wise to consider what other people's personality types may be, how they are thinking, and how they might be perceiving what you are saying and how you are leading. While it is unwise to try to peg every person's type solely by their behavior, the point is to be aware that behavior likely has its roots in their natural personality type. Remember, it is not about the type as much as about the approach employed by the person. And I must also point out that most personality type systems are descriptive, not prescriptive. More about that later.

I had another enlightening experience with a team member who tests almost the exact opposite on the MBTI assessment scale. I type as ENFJ. He types as ISTJ. He and I worked together for years, and while we always approached a question from a different perspective and through a different set of lenses, we invariably would come to the same conclusion. Our different approaches helped us realize that we were affirming each other's decisions because of our different approaches to issues. Bottom line: having a diversity of types in the decision-making processes strengthens an organization's function. That is a theme that is wise for all leaders to follow as we progress down the leadership road.

There is another lesson to be learned from my experience. Any type can work with any other type, as long as at least one of the persons is willing to consider and appreciate what the other person's type brings to the table. Being of the same type may seem comfortable as you understand each other's perspective, but if two people are thinking alike, why do you need both of them to participate? On the other hand, a person with the opposite typing of your dichotomous pairs can be viewed as annoying or can be valued for opening up different thoughts on a topic.

What I also came to learn was that depending on the power structure in the room, some people modified their approach, at least for a while. Most seasoned people can modify their behavior and not participate "true to type," based on the setting and what is at stake. I also experienced this shift from a different perspective. As a new dean, I was very uncomfortable when interacting with all the much more experienced deans and administrators. When I completed my first MBTI assessment in that environment, I typed as strongly introverted. Repeated assessments in later years showed that I type as an extrovert.

Why the shift? I realize now that I was modifying my approach, even unconsciously, curtailing my naturally outgoing personality due to feeling so inexperienced. I got over that!

The other important point to remember is that regardless of how well modulated and modified the seasoned leader and team member might be, when put under extreme stress and pressure with high stakes, it is the rare individual who does NOT revert to their original type. So, watch out when you really put the pressure on, as you may find some different and less-effective approaches/responses and perspectives start to pop up from the group members. And from you! The rocky patch of road in leadership can shake a leader to the core if you don't have a good set of shock absorbers.

There is another interesting point about different personality types and approaches. You know what annoys you about other personality types and approaches? Be careful, as the things that annoy you may be reflecting aspects of your own personality and approach. A wise person once said that others are mirrors of you. You will see what you love or hate in yourself, in the behavior of others. Which is why it is often not solving your problem to move from one work setting to another. "There" is no better than "here," especially when I must bring myself and all my quirks and foibles with me from "there" to "here." Sometimes the lack of a leadership roadmap results in the novice leader going in circles! Think about it.

I am recommending that you consider taking the MBTI and also the DiSC assessments listed in the Resources at the end of this chapter, as they are the most well studied in leadership settings. As you are aware that there are different types, you will benefit from spending a little time perusing the literature that explains how each type likes to function; what are the best leadership approaches to work with each type, especially based on your type; what kind of culture the leader's type creates; and what kind of culture develops in response to the predominant type in the team. Even if you don't have time to take the assessments, remember what Yogi Berra supposedly said: "You can observe a lot by just watching."

Anais Nin is credited with saying: "We don't see things as THEY are, we see things as WE are!"

Steven Covey (2004) made a similar point: "The way we see the problem IS the problem." And yes, it can be hard to work with people who see the world differently from how you see it. It can also be an excellent learning opportunity. More on these points in Perspectives, Chapter 4.

NOW! Quit guessing what type you are and take either the short version or the fully analyzed versions of these most common assessment tools.

Takeaways for the Wise Physician Leader

We are not all alike; we do not bring the same approaches to the table. But all personality types have important contributions to make. Diversity is a good thing! The good news is that some very smart people have figured this out long ago and have developed categories and assessment tools to determine the categories. Take advantage of the personality assessment tools available to learn about yourself and come to learn, appreciate, and welcome others' approaches and perspectives. Your road will be much smoother and result in more effective leadership if you do so!

Questions

1. Have you experienced a situation where your perception of an issue differed from another person's view? How did that influence the outcome of the issue? Why did the other person perceive the issue differently than you? What personality approach might that person have brought to the issue?

2. Have you ever seen a scenario where the extrovert in the group drove the direction of the discussion of an issue? And that direction may have been facilitated/exacerbated by a leader who did not seek to bring out other perspectives. How did that promote or inhibit the best solution?

3. Have you encountered a statistics-driven individual who is always asking "give me the data"? How did that approach facilitate or slow down the process? When was that approach necessary to move the analysis forward? When did that approach serve to divert the discussion from the real issue at hand? Could that have been the intent?

4. What have you learned about how you personally approach a problem or situation? How does your natural approach assist or hinder the understanding of the options? What situations are more comfortable for you? What situations do you try to avoid, either intentionally or inadvertently?

5. Consider a situation where you do not know the other individuals. Do you squelch your natural-type approach until you see the direction of the group? Or do you follow your usual type reaction, which you have employed in a similar situation? How will those choices facilitate or hinder the situation?

Take a break for a minute and consider this. If you are going to get the most benefit from this or any leadership study, you need to periodically reflect on your performance with the person who is watching you in every leadership situation, you! This appendix will guide you through a short daily/weekly reflection exercise. Additionally, as you read through each subsequent chapter in this book, bounce back to this reflection exercise and plan how you will regularly use this guide to facilitate your leadership development progression, based on analyzing what worked and what could have been handled more effectively.

Appendix: Reflection Exercise

I recommend reflection or thinking as a helpful exercise to prepare for each roadmap chapter.

"Thinking? Really? I'm a doctor! I think all the time!"

Yes, I get that, but I'm recommending a focused, organized logical system. Spending even a few minutes at the end of the day reviewing that day's interactions will be instructional. We tend to spend time analyzing why something didn't work; we are less likely to analyze why something did work. Both outcomes deserve equal attention When something doesn't work well, we tend to ask this question of ourselves: "What were you thinking?" We also need to ask ourselves, "What WEREN'T you thinking?"

- What worked well, and why? (General Overview)
- Did I listen more or talk more? Chapter 2, Communication
- Was I able to move forward the pivotal points/comments/issues that popped up that could have gone either way, by clarifying definitions, asking more questions, and being careful about inferences? How well did I read body language of the others, even in virtual meetings? Chapter 3, Communication Techniques
- How did my perspectives and those of others in the encounter regarding the situation facilitate or hamper the resolution of the situation? Chapter 4, Perspectives
- How well did the decision-making part of the meeting go? If that part of the meeting did work well, what did I do that enhanced the likelihood? Or the reverse? Chapters 5–6, Decision-Making.
- Did I contribute positively or negatively to my team and others around me? Did I set an example for others? Chapter 7, Character and Ethics.
- What could I have done differently to make someone feel better after an interaction with me than they felt before? Chapter 8, Relationships.
- How well did I maintain composure under stress? Chapter 9, Negotiations.
- Did I bring my own unstated "rules" to the conversation? Chapter 10, Conflict Management.
- Was I able to effectively employ proven principles and techniques of persuasion to move the discussion? Chapter 11.
- When seeking to move a change, did I start by establishing a sense of urgency? Chapter 12.

These are also helpful questions to review when watching another leader, novice or experienced, and see what worked and didn't work. Most importantly, why?

I wish I could say that I don't have to conduct this analysis myself. I wish I could say that I have mastered every point in every chapter and can achieve the optimal outcome every time. But that doesn't describe my approach – and I dare say it doesn't describe that of any other physician leader that I know, either.

Realistically, I also wish I had the time to conduct a full reflection of my day as a leader, every day. I just don't have the time and you won't, either. However, every one of us can do a gut check, which only takes a couple of minutes. Either "day went well" or "sheesh!" Take a couple notes from the "went well" days and from the "sheesh" days and do the reflection exercise when you have a little time to dedicate to your leadership progress. Believe me, it will pay you dividends many times over.

So, let's get started! Full speed ahead!

Resources

There are many resources on all these personality analysis approaches. Here are some of the books and the websites.

Briggs Myers, I., and Myers, P. (1980). *Gifts Differing: Understanding Personality Type.* Ann Arbor, MI: Davies-Black Publishing (www.personalitypathways.com).

Briggs Myers, I., revised by Kirby, L. Myers K., (1993). *Introduction to Type,* 5th ed. Palo Alto, CA: Consulting Psychologists Press, Inc.

Canfield, A. (2018). *The Enneagram of Personality: Why Discovering Your Unique Personality Type Is Essential for Your Personal Growth.* Stone Ridge, NY: Enneagram Institute (www.enneagraminstitute.com).

Rath, T. (2007). *Strengths Finder 2.0.* New York: Gallup Press (www.gallup.com).

Sugerman, J. (2011). *The 8 Dimensions of Leadership: DiSC Strategies for Becoming a Better Leader.* San Francisco, CA: Berrett-Koehler Publishing (www.institutesuccess.com/Free/Assessment).

The following sources are also useful leadership guides.

Bennis, W. (2009). *On Becoming a Leader* (4th ed.) New York: Basic Books.

Covey, S. R. (2004). *The 7 Habits of Highly Successful People: Powerful Lessons in Personal Change*. New York: Free Press.

Lao-Tzu (2000). *Tao Te Ching (Book of the Way)* (trans. S. Mitchell). New York: Harper Perennial.

Plato (399 BCE). *Apology* (trans. B. Jowett). Originally published in 1892; public domain.

Watkins, M. (2013) *The First 90 Days: Proven Strategies for Getting Up to Speed Faster and Smarter, Updated and Expanded,* Boston: Harvard Business School Publishing.

Chapter TWO

Communication

Learning principles of communication is one of the most important skills for a leader to master.

> *"Wait a minute! I thought you just said that knowing yourself was the most important aspect of leadership!"*

Well, yes and yes. The first big challenge to master is communication. You cannot be a leader if you don't understand how to effectively communicate. But you cannot even learn how to communicate if you don't know yourself and your personality/communication style first. It's a chicken-and-egg kind of thing.

Principles of Communication

Here is a crucial statement about communication: "The single biggest problem in communication is the illusion that it has taken place" (White 1950). Truer words were never spoken.

We will consider four principles of communication:

1. Know the definitions.
2. Ask questions.
3. Use the ladder of inference.
4. Understand person and persona.

Know the Definitions

The first principle is the importance of our perceptions and understanding of *definitions*.

I was going to a reception at Rush University Medical Center in December-frigid Chicago. Unfortunately, the published address was not exactly specific. Rush University has a series of academic buildings sitting in the middle of a section of businesses, and any one building is hard to tell from any other building, as to its purpose. I walked past several buildings, and finally gave up on my skills of discernment, at least as far as buildings were concerned. I found a building with an information desk, and when it was my turn to speak to the attendant, I asked where the reception was being held and how to get there. It is important to this story to know that I did not know the name of the room where the conference was being held. I now understand that the attendant thought I did know the name of the conference center. The friendly attendant did find the reception location on his list of events and said the room name quickly. What I heard was, "It's in the Sir Conference Center." Not only did I not know where that was, I had no idea how to spell that name so that I could look for that name on any sign. So, I tried to be very polite as I asked him to pronounce the name again. I heard the same name. With no other option, I asked if he could spell it? With a long pause and slight hint of disdain, he said, "C-O-N-F-E-R-E-N-C-E Center." "No, I mean the first word in the name." Another pause. "S-E-A-R-L-E." At first, I thought he was joking, but he was dead serious. From his perspective, the conference center was so famous, that he could not imagine anyone would not know the name "Searle." The problem was exacerbated by the fact that Searle's two syllables are often slurred into one. (By the way, the drug company of the same name has long vanished from the American scene.)

We used very common words in our conversation. The words had clear definitions. The definitions were accurate, but the interpretation was different. The words had very different implications and consequences. Doctors, we deal with this dilemma all the time!! But we know how to translate the terms in medicine. Stay with me through another example!

While I was president of the American Osteopathic Association (AOA), the Institute of Medicine (now the National Academy of Science, Engineering and Medicine) prepared a long treatise on the "Future of Nursing: Leading Change, Advancing Health" published in October 2010. Admittedly, this is my perspective as a physician, but the impression I got from this paper was that the nursing profession was being proposed as being capable of providing what was needed for the future of US health care with over 3 million nurses already in place. Yes, the title was "The Future of Nursing," but there was little mention of the role of physicians, and in my reading of the document, the nursing profession was presented as capable of filling a majority of roles in providing medical care. I was not the only person who gleaned this perspective from that paper and felt it painted an incomplete picture of the future of the bigger picture of medicine and health care in the United States, which includes nurses and doctors, among other professions. Several physician organizations (AMA, AAP, AAFP, AOA) joined together and wrote a letter to the editor of *New England Journal of Medicine* about our perspective on this document. It will undoubtedly be the only time I will ever be published in the NEJM. I fully understand that the nursing profession is working through issues of function and structure. While we all felt that the nursing profession does and will continue to play an enormous and crucial role in providing health care in the United States, this treatise felt simply unbalanced from the physician perspective. Subsequently, the Robert Wood Johnson Foundation (RWJF) invited representatives of six physician organizations and six nursing organizations to a series of workshop sessions to see if we could hash out some of the differences between our perspectives. In summary, we met in four sessions over more than a year, totaling about 16 days. RWJF brought in an excellent facilitation team, who announced they had worked on the Middle East peace negotiations under President Jimmy Carter, which led to the Middle East Peace Accords being signed with Abba Eban and Yasser Arafat. I joked that it was too bad that they had not worked on something as difficult as getting doctors and nurses to agree! I never included the rest of this story as it wasn't pertinent to my point. So I shouldn't imply that I'm going to finish the story. The facilitation team did a fantastic job, tackling the real issues and getting all the perspectives on the table.

The point of this story in the context of communication is as follows: At one point the 12 participants were discussing the proper role of nurses in providing health care. One of the nurses made the point "We are independent, you know." The immediate response from the physicians? "No, you are not independent." You can imagine the arguments and subsequent deterioration of the conversations from there. This discussion went on for a while. Neither side budged. Finally, the facilitator said, "What do you mean by independent?" The nurses stated that they were independently licensed and were afforded the ability and further, were required to take responsibility for their actions. They were appropriately authorized and required to question any order, any dosage, any plan that did not appear to be correct. They have independent licenses. You could hear the collective sigh of insight and relief in the room. The physicians' definition of independent encompassed the ability of a physician to practice without supervision and to conduct the practice of medicine solely under her/his own recognizance. Both the nurses and doctors were using the same word, just using different definitions/ implications.

Ask Questions

The second principle along this road is to *ask questions*.

First, to put this thought into perspective, answer this question yourself. What is your least favorite chief complaint/concern from a patient? Now I know the answer to that question depends on your specialty area of practice. However, I would submit that almost any specialty must deal with some variation of this type of chief complaint/concern: "I'm fatigued, weak, tired, or in pain." It could be a primary complaint or a response to some treatment as a side effect.

Why is this such a challenging chief complaint? Because it is so vague! What does it mean? What is the patient referring to? In my practice experience, *dizzy* has very different meanings to patients. It could mean the sensation of personally spinning, or room spinning, or being light-headed, or feeling they were about to fall down. So how do you make the diagnosis? Of course, you know the answer: you ask questions, LOTS of questions. The application of this principle to leadership situations should be very easy to make, but it is not. Remember, it's not what's said, it's what's heard.

And further, it is what is meant and interpreted. Every doctor knows they do not know what "tired" means to a particular patient. No doctor would say, "Oh yes, you are tired! That always and definitively means you are anemic!" Maybe that is the cause, but questions and analysis must precede that diagnosis. (Most recently, the issue of interpreting a complaint of pain has drawn a lot of attention. The patient is not well served by a quick response of an opioid prescription without a thoughtful assessment with appropriate questions. Granted this is just one facet of the opioid crisis.)

In the leadership arena, very few leaders are intuitively able to accurately assess a plan or suggestion at first blush, either. We know what those words mean, right? It should be simple, right? Just listen to the words. Much more important is listening to what perceptions are behind the definition of those words. Do not forget the high-level talks that were almost derailed simply by the unclear use of the word *independent*.

Here is the problem: We know to ask questions to understand the vague complaint of our patients. But we seldom think to ask questions to understand the vague comment heard in leadership – because we don't realize it is vague. The speaker knows what the words mean. The leader knows what the words mean. The only way to find out if they *agree* on the meanings is to ASK QUESTIONS!

Another reason we don't ask good questions is because we can easily default to being reductionists. We will pick apart and study one process at a time, even though we know these processes do not happen in isolation. As osteopathic physicians, we are taught to look at the whole person. That is still not easy when you are in a busy practice and lots of patients are waiting for care. There is an interesting theory about possible ways that trees in a grove may "communicate." This perspective is from Suzanne Simard's work, quoted in "The Whispering of the Trees" (Grant 2018). The trees are seen as having a large underground communication system of roots that crisscross with their neighboring trees. The roots are detecting water levels, chemical levels, and insect infestations, and they "share" that information with other trees. There are some interesting parallels with our osteopathic "whole person" philosophy.

As a leader, be sure to ask open-ended questions. Asking yes/no questions does not allow for clarification and description. When the other person makes a statement, ask for more concrete information, such as, "What exactly does that mean to you?" Or "Tell me more," or "What does that look like to you?" Definitions are critical and so easily misperceived. The only time to consider avoiding open-ended questions as you proceed down the road is in a tense situation where that approach will leave too much wiggle room to either avoid the question or introduce extraneous material that derails the conversation.

Further, be very careful that you do not use questions to cross-examine the other person! At a minimum, it is frustrating, and beyond that, it can be insulting. And certainly, do not make statements disguised as questions. We have all been in meetings where a person is pretending to ask a question but uses the floor to make a statement or state a position.

After receiving the question's answer, it is frequently helpful to paraphrase for clarity. This serves two purposes. First, especially if you are the only person with the microphone, this allows everyone to hear the question. Second, it can clarify what question is being asked. We have all heard this comment: "So what I hear you saying is..." Sometimes it feels a bit condescending, especially when what was said seems pretty stupid. However, when the leader is truly trying to understand the earlier statement, it can serve to check for understanding, especially if the statement has been long and somewhat convoluted. Maybe that was not even what the person wanted to say; maybe the person did not really intend to include all those potential implications. At the very least, it shows that you have heard what was said, whether agreed with or not, and have respected and honored the speaker. When you are the subject of the questioning, you may choose to answer opaquely, which protects your options. On the other hand, answering transparently promotes more options. And on the other side of the road, that is the kind of wiggle room you as the questioner do not want to allow to slide by, unexamined.

Use the Ladder of Inference

The third principle of communication you need to understand very clearly is called the *ladder of inference,* as described by Chris Argyris (1990).

This is a communication principle that works very well for medicine, in fact is required for medicine. However, using his ladder of inference structure in a leadership situation in the same way you do in medicine is very dangerous, if you are not aware that you are using it. Below are the five rungs/steps of the ladder. The bottom and beginning first step or rung of the ladder is presented first, #1, with the top rung of the ladder of inference as #5.

#1 Available facts and data as observed (bottom rung or first step).

#2 Selected facts for further consideration (next rung up, etc.).

#3 Paraphrase for the meaning that turns the selected facts into a specific implication.

#4 Name or assumptions of what is happening, which turns that implication into an assumption of intent.

#5 Conclusions that explain and validate what is happening with little observable data at that point (top rung).

Here is another way to look at the ladder of inference and how it works in medicine:

#1 We begin with all the observable data, restricted to just the actual event that was seen (bottom rung). Here is what you observe:

The patient had a new and more shuffling gait as he came into the examining room.

He is not his usual smiling self.

His belt was taken in two more notches than where it had previously become well-worn.

He is slumping more on the exam table than he usually does.

His wedding ring nearly falls off his finger.

He smells of tobacco, as an avowed nonsmoker.

His shirt collar sags open, a size too big.

His clothes smell musty, have not been washed recently.

#2 Since we cannot pay attention to and notice everything, we must select some of the observable data and ignore some of the rest of it; that is how our brains work. (Second rung of the ladder from the bottom.)

The patient had a new, more shuffling gait as he came into the examining room.

His belt was taken in two more notches than where it had previously become well-worn.

His wedding ring nearly falls off his finger.

His shirt collar sags open, a size too big.

#3 We must put the descriptive words into our own words, which may
   or may not be the full picture (remember the caution about assuming
   which definitions are being used).
   Shuffling gait
   Change in belt length, smaller waist circumference
   Shirt too big
   Wedding ring too big

#4 Our brains continue the interpretation process by characterizing
   what is happening as belonging to a more general category of event.
   Further, we explain what is happening by drawing on our stock of
   causal theories and evaluate the data and subsequent interpretation as
   good or bad.
   He looks like he has lost weight and is weak, not walking with
   any strength.

#5 We then draw conclusions based on the full picture "as we see it and
   interpret it." My physician interpretation:
   He has lost his appetite, which does not appear intentional, and may
   have a malignancy, at least a wasting process.

The use of the *ladder of inference* is an important part of how we practice
medicine. As soon as you as the doctor see the patient, you make the observations noted above, probably in about a minute or two. You take in the
observable data, select what is most important or has changed significantly,
project some possible meanings to the various things observed, make some
assumptions of what could be causing those changes, and draw conclusions
of what is the most likely underlying cause, what we know to be the differential diagnosis list.

So here is the problem with using the ladder of inference in the leadership setting as opposed to its very different usefulness in medicine. In
medicine, we have been taught the content of the subject and have studied
and have practiced making these inferences and implications. This education is based on years of study and experience relating to the most likely
implications. Not so in leadership. Stay with me on this point while I create
a leadership demonstration of the ladder.

Here is a little exercise I have used to teach this concept. I select four
people to come to the front of the room of learners and to wait patiently
with no other instructions. I send one additional person out of the room,
step out with them, and quietly give the following instruction: "Come

into the room and give the first person in the line a very warm hug and have a brief engaging welcoming conversation, just about 10 seconds in length. Do the same with the second and fourth person in the line. Obviously, the third person is skipped, not acknowledged in any way. End of the scenario." The participants follow these instructions. At the conclusion of that scenario, all participants are applauded by the observing group and then sit down. Now I turn to the audience, "What was that all about? What happened there?" They give wild guesses of what was going on; the longer the guessing, the wilder the guesses – the welcomer and person #3 were enemies, they were trying to build different coalitions, for example. The funniest inference? They were involved in a romantic relationship and did not want anyone to know about it!

Then I introduce the *ladder of inference* concept and push the group to go down to level/rung one, describing the concretely observable data. Someone finally gets the idea and states, you saw one person come in and greet three of the four persons in the room. That is all that can be observed. It then becomes very clear to the group that we all quickly jump several rungs up the ladder of inference as we come up with the explanations for that observed behavior. We cannot help ourselves! And then I ask them to think about situations they have seen in leadership where they make assumptions in real life.

So, what was the back story of the scenario being portrayed above, for illustration purposes? The welcomer and person #3 had already met at this meeting and already warmly greeted each other. OK, I understand that the demonstration is not true to the scenario as in the real scenario, person #3 would have known why they were not being greeted. But remember, you as an outside observer of this set of encounters, would have had no demonstrated evidence of why person #3 was not greeted, thus the set-up and real-life example of the **ladder of inference**.

In leadership situations, we immediately start to make guesses about what we have observed. The problem is, we don't have enough information to accurately jump up those inference ladder rungs. We might be right; it is just that we usually don't have enough background to make valid assumptions and thus accurate conclusions. It is not a problem to make these inferences; it is a problem not to realize we are making inferences, and to think those inferences are accurate. Watch out!! Roadblock ahead!

There are pitfalls of making low inferences and making high inferences. Making only a low-level inference about an observed situation will likely leave you missing what is really going on. Making only a high-level inference about an observed situation may lead you to the correct interpretation of what was happening behind the scenes. It can also lead to a very incorrect conclusion that is not even close to what was happening. Suffice it to say that we make high-level inferences much more often than low-level ones. And when the stakes are high, I can guarantee we make high-level inferences.

Understand Person and Persona

The fourth principle of communication that is important to keep in mind is the concept of *person and persona*.

When you are a leader, you need to understand that you are then a "person" and also have a "persona." A what?? You are still Karen Nichols, a private individual entitled to her opinions and her methods of communication. And now you are also Dr. Nichols, the leader of this group expressing opinions. As a private person, you are entitled to your opinions. When you are in the role as a leader, the opinions you express are reflecting the group/organization in which you are leading. This differentiation is even more critical in the world of social media. If you include a list of your current leadership roles in your social media accounts, any communications in that media outlet will be seen as reflecting the opinions of those organizations in which you have a leadership role. I have seen more than one person express a strong and polarizing opinion in social media that does not reflect well on their leadership role. I must admit that I have made some mental notes about individuals whose comments would be perceived as inflammatory in a leadership situation. Such comments on religion and politics come to mind, especially in the current political climate.

I remember a conversation with a newly elected student leader at CCOM. I had earlier met with the group of all the newly elected leaders and discussed how they were now representatives of CCOM, wherever they went and whatever they did. This particular student leader came to my office a few days later to discuss that conversation. Her big question, "When can I just be me? When can I cut loose? When can I just be who I am?"

My answer: "When you are in a place where no one knows who you are – and how can you be sure where that might be?" She was not comfortable that she had just adopted the persona of a student leader, which carried expectations for behavior. Hard lesson for her to learn, and for some physician leaders as well.

Further, frequently we wear more than one leadership "hat." It is helpful to clarify which hat you are wearing with a specific comment in a meeting. It is important, yes necessary, to say "from my perspective as a dean…" or "when I was in private practice…" Those caveats also clarify that you are or are not speaking from the perspective of your leadership role in that meeting. Remember, as you go down that road, it may not be possible to eliminate the perception of your association with a particular role you hold.

Another aspect of person/persona differences that must be watched is how you address the members of the group. As Dr. Nichols, you know some of these people by their first names, but not all. As Dr. Nichols you could lead the meeting and call on those you know, by their first names. And then call on those you don't know by their formal titles. That sends all kinds of messages – wrong messages. Using first names for some can diminish their status in the group, while using titles implies deference to those other members of the group. On the other hand, using first names for some in the group can also imply that you have more confidence in their opinions because you already know them. The "person" of Karen Nichols can call people by whatever name is appropriate. The "persona" of the Leader Dr. Nichols must call all people by the same naming convention, preferably by titles. Implications of this point for gender equity will be discussed in Chapter 14.

Appreciative Inquiry

The appreciative inquiry is a highly regarded communication approach. I will illustrate the approach with this situation. When I was president of one of the organizations I have been honored to serve, the membership committee chair asked to meet with me about a new idea. He had read about another organization that stopped charging dues! It developed a menu of member services and charged individually for them instead of a flat membership fee. No question, this was one of the stupidest ideas I had ever heard. Much of what any organization does falls into general support categories that members are challenged to appreciate in advance, at least not until after they need them. So they are not likely to choose to prospectively pay for them, but they are critical services and need funding. But the person proposing this idea was also one of the most thoughtful chairs I had ever had. There was definite leadership potential there. Having recently read about the appreciative inquiry, I could not think of a better situation in which to try it out. The basic idea is to withhold judgment as you ask questions to gain a better understanding. The focus of employing the appreciative inquiry approach is in how you ask the questions.

I launched into the inquiry model roadmap as follows:

Step One. "What is the idea/proposal?"
So, tell me more about how this concept would work. What kinds of things could you charge for? How much would you charge? How often would you charge that person? What kinds of things would people most likely pay for?
Step Two. "What could the idea/proposal be used for/develop into?"
How else could this concept be developed? How could it be rolled out? Could there be a pilot? Could there be a partial implementation to see how it worked?
Step Three. "What else could the idea/proposal develop into/be used for?"
Could this concept be used in a partial way at our convention by breaking the registration into single-day segments and see how that worked? Could this approach be implemented for some of our most popular documents while simultaneously lowering the dues amount just a bit, in order to see how many choose to purchase the documents separate from the dues?
Step Four. "What will the next steps be?"
What has been the experience in other organizations? How did they move to this structure? What were the financial implications for them? Have other organizations developed a set of best practices for implementation? Have other organizations implemented and then retracted such a plan? What was the impact of that?

The idea/proposal is not being attacked or judged, it is being analyzed, appreciatively. Ideas and proposals may have just popped up or, alternatively, may have been well thought out, but the point is to look for the useful nugget that resides in every idea, even if the presented approach is not feasible in that format.

I love the message that these two different approaches to a response will engender.

1. "I don't see how this can work. Go back and try again." OR
2. "I don't understand all the aspects of this idea. However, when someone of your value to this organization comes up with an idea like this, it is worth my time to review it with you."

Much nicer!! And who knows, maybe that person really does have a good idea! I am still following the roadmap myself! Who knew??

A caution about communicating by email. Generational differences can trip you up. Some people expect greetings, closings and titles. Others consider those a waste of time. The road map tells you to follow the example of the authority figure you are communicating with!

Takeaways for the Wise Physician Leader

Learning principles of communication is crucial to accomplishing your goals in a leadership situation. In medicine, we use questions and definitions to drill down to the correct diagnosis. Those approaches serve the same purposes in the leadership situations. The additional aspect of the definitions for words used in a leadership situation are the different perceptions of those definitions. The skilled physician also employs the ladder of inference in assessing and monitoring patients, even if that specific descriptive phrase is seldom used to describe this aspect of medical care. In leadership, we often utilize the same ladder of inference, which unfortunately can start us down a very slippery slope! OK, mixed metaphors there! Also, not a wise approach to employ in leadership, if not used with understanding and some healthy skepticism. In medicine, we know how to read a patient and how to make helpful inferences. Not so in leadership. Finally, understanding the importance of person/persona is usually not an issue for the physician, as the role of the physician in society is generally well understood. But in the leadership arena, slipping back and forth between the person and the persona or flipping those hats without clarity is another dangerous trap to avoid as you move down the road.

Scenarios

Look at these three scenarios:

1. You are at a national meeting and you see two people from different states quietly talking in the corner before the meeting starts.
2. At the same meeting, you see physicians from two different medical groups having a drink together at a more secluded bar.
3. You are in your office and see a physician from another state enter the practice manager's office just a week after the announcement of the practice expansion with a new leadership position opening.

What do you surmise is happening in each of these three scenarios? And further, what could be happening in these scenarios? And the basic question, what did you actually observe? How far up the ladder of inference are you going?

Questions

1. Jane and Bill have brought two different proposals to the meeting for your leadership team to consider. Both proposals have good points. Jane concludes her presentation with the comment, "This proposal truly reflects what this organization stands for." Everyone nods and her proposal is accepted. As the implementation rolls out, several steps in the process feel discordant to your team. How could you have drilled down to what Jane meant by "what this organization stands for"? Now what will you have to do to get back on track?
2. In your leadership meeting, you are asked your opinion about the various options for speed of implementation of the new project. You express an opinion off the top of your head about the advisability for a general need for greater speed of implementation, as opposed to a

slower approach. Later, you overhear the staff telling other team members, "Dr. xxx said we have to speed up our processes." That is not what you meant; you were just making an off-hand comment. Can you ever truly make an off-hand comment as a physician leader?

3. What situations have you observed where two different definitions of a word were being used by two people in a discussion? What happened to the discussion and outcome? Were the different definitions ever identified or even recognized?

4. When have you found that you did not fully understand the situation at hand when you thought you did, and the lack of questioning of and by the participants led to a less-than-optimal result? How could you have used appreciative inquiry questions to avoid this pitfall?

5. Have you ever responded with your personal opinion only to realize later that your comments were interpreted as representative of your organization? What issues were created due to that interpretation?

Resources

Argyris, C. (1990). *Overcoming Organizational Defenses: Facilitating Organizational Learning.* Needham Heights, MA: Allyn and Bacon.

Bolton, R. (1986). *People Skills: How to Assert Yourself, Listen to Others, and Resolve Conflicts.* New York: Touchstone.

Grant, R. (2018). The Whispering of the Trees. *Smithsonian,* March.

Hoppe, M. H. (2006). *Active Listening: Improve Your Ability to Listen and Lead.* Greensboro, NC: Center for Creative Leadership.

White, W. H. (1950). Fortune 42:77–83.

Chapter THREE
Techniques of Communication

Early in my dean career, I was presented with an issue whereby the OMS 3 class had hosted a fund raiser selling diploma frames to the OMS 4 graduating class. Unfortunately, the frames had not arrived by the anticipated date. I requested a meeting with the OMS 3 class president. When he came to my office, I introduced myself and laid out the issue with my extreme disappointment in that situation. I went on and on about the unacceptable outcome we were facing. By the time I was finished, he was figuratively blasted against the wall. Finally, he said his first words, "Do you want to hear my side of the story?" Whoa, did I feel small! I just blew through the first technique of communication, listening. Not only did I not follow the roadmap, I went off the shoulder and down into a gully!

In this chapter, we will cover three techniques of communication and then four critical words or word pairs.

Three Techniques of Communication

Listen

Let's start with the technique applicable to the situation above: LISTEN! Dr. Joyce Brothers, psychologist, columnist, and best-selling author, was heard to have said that "listening, not imitation, may be the sincerest form of flattery." The Dalai Lama has said, "When you talk, you are only repeating what you already know: when you listen, you may learn something new."

"Well really?? Of course, we must listen."

Listening is very hard for me personally as I like to talk, and I have a lot to say. Most of us "pseudo-listen" as we are planning out what we intend to say in response, or what point we plan to make next. We may be "listening," but we are really just looking for an obvious break in the "diatribe" coming from the other person so we can blurt out our truly important, insightful, and pithy comments to set the other person straight. Real listening requires we not only hear the words but also stop our own planning for the next words/steps – carefully listening not only to clearly hear what is being said but also to assess our own reactions to what the other person is saying. If we truly listen, the next words we had been planning to say may not turn out to be the best ones.

To listen well, we must hear the words and the silence between the words. Sometimes the most powerful words and concepts are the ones not said. So, watch for the *pregnant pause,* defined as not speaking when the normal of flow of conversation would indicate it is time for another comment. For example, let us say a particular aspect of the conversation in the meeting has been tense. Now no one is saying anything. You, as the leader, also must just wait! It is hard for everyone to tolerate that silent space. It is human nature to fill that vacuum with some words – just do not let them be yours. If you talk, you will only hear what you already think. If you let someone else talk, you might learn something.

Read the Body Language

Second technique: Read their body language. This is a huge issue with virtual meetings, as some don't share their video, among other meeting no-nos. "Only 7 percent of communication is what you're saying – the rest is your tone of voice, expression, and body language," according to

Kimberly Alyn (Phillips and Alyn 2011). Again, every doctor knows to do this with every patient:

- The patient whose bravado and bluster suddenly dissipates when s/he gets to the real matter of concern.
- The teen in your medical office who sits with crossed arms while their parent relates the complaint.
- The patient who literally turns away from you in the chair, demonstrating reluctance to go any further in the discussion.

The exact same examples of body language apply to the speaker in the leadership situation. The speaker is telling you more than they think they are or maybe even intend to. If it doesn't sound true, it isn't. There is a reason for what people say, but it is usually not the reason they think.

A new staffer in our office seemed to have trouble connecting with our patients. We had several complaints from patients that he did not listen, cut them off, and didn't convey respect to them as people. I took the opportunity to plan a little training session for all our staff on patient interaction. Maybe all would benefit from a little refresher, and maybe the new person was just being misperceived. I personally had not seen any inappropriate interactions with patients. All the staffers sat in a circle in our lobby. Except the staffer in question. He did not pull his chair into the circle, he made our circle into more of a pumpkin with a stem, and he was the stem. And he turned his chair more to the wall than toward the group. And his arms were crossed over his chest, which fully matched the scowl on his face. He objected to the exercise, did not answer the softball questions, and it got worse from there. Needless to say, he was not an employee of the practice much longer.

Know When to Interrupt

The third technique I want you to consider is *when and if to interrupt someone.* I do not think I have ever seen this topic discussed or written about until very recently. I would venture to say that if you asked the next 10 people you see whether it is appropriate to interrupt someone in a conversation, most would say no. I will share two scenarios I experienced that bring a different perspective.

I had an interesting experience in a conversation with a program director at a large hospital where I was hoping to obtain some internal medicine student rotation slots. The program director was gracious and welcomed me to his office. I introduced myself and clarified my purpose, of which he was likely already aware. He started to talk. And talk. And talk. And talk. He probably talked nonstop for at least 30 minutes without appearing to take a breath, ask me a question, or request my perspective. He just kept talking! I couldn't get a word in edgewise. Every time I attempted to venture into the conversation either to agree or bring up an additional point, he just kept on talking. Very rude! Finally, he abruptly stopped talking in the middle of his sentence, looked at me and said, "If you don't say something, I'm just going to keep on talking!"

From my perspective, he was being rude and not letting me talk. If I had interrupted him, my interpretation was that I would be guilty of being rude as well. From his perspective as expressed through that comment, it appeared to me that he expected me to interrupt him, and if I didn't, he interpreted that I was being too deferent, and my points were not worthy of his consideration. Let's just say the conversation did not go well. Was this a man/woman thing? A different home environment or upbringing thing? A different set of rules that are employed only in the medical world? I'll never know. And we didn't get those rotations, either.

Subsequently, Jessica Bennett (2015) writes about this in "How Not to Be 'Manterrupted' in Meetings." She gives this practice, a name and a definition: "an unnecessary interruption of a woman, usually by a man."

The second experience I had was when I went into practice in Mesa, Arizona. There were about 180 doctors on staff, and I was the third woman. The first two were in the fields of pathology and OB/GYN and were seldom seen out of their respective departments. So, when I went into the doctors' dining room, I was entering a room with up to a couple dozen male doctors sitting at round tables. I got my lunch and joined them. The conversations continued. It seemed appropriate to take part in the conversation, but I never could get a word in edgewise. I finally learned by watching the flow of the other doctors' conversations that if I was going to get to speak, I had to interrupt someone else and take over the floor to make my point.

The only way I could interject my comments was to interrupt – which I did – and then continue to talk over him (it was always a man) – which I did not do – that would be rude! Or so I perceived. I eventually learned that since I did not talk over whomever was speaking and force my way into the conversation, he didn't view that as a "valid and successful" interruption, so he kept on talking! I learned how to interrupt and got quite good at it.

Now the interesting thing I have since noticed is that not all groups conduct conversations that way. Once I was in a different group and found myself interrupting the conversation as I had learned to do, which effectively stopped the conversation. I got the clear sense that I had been rude. Very odd! It was not always a male/female predominant group, either. So, I have learned to watch, listen, and weigh the situation before deciding whether interrupting is expected or inappropriate. I also discovered it was not the last time that I had to learn that interrupting (though rude in my life experience) was a required aspect of making my points in some discussions, but not all. Sometimes that roadmap has detours to still get you where you want to go!

Words and Word Pairs: What to Use, What to Avoid

Now let's look at words that we use in communications that need to be chosen carefully.

I or You

First, we are going to review the choice of two words you can choose to begin a sentence:

■ "I" or "You."

There are two different situations in which you must consider the use of the word *I* and the word *you*. These comments refer to starting a sentence with one word or the other. The situations are either nonconfrontational or confrontational.

In the *nonconfrontational* discussion, especially where you are hoping to influence/persuade a specific outcome, it is best to use the word *I* as little as possible. In this case, the word *I* draws attention to myself. Keeping the self-aggrandizement (boasting) to an absolute minimum demonstrates humility, respect, and a healthy dose of positivity. The old joke? "So, enough about me, what do *you* think about me?"

"Enough, truly!"

In the *confrontational* discussion, especially when seeking to discuss a sensitive topic with varied perceptions of right and wrong (the other person is wrong and you are right, of course), it is best to start sentences with the word *I*.

"Really? I thought you just got done saying not to use the word "I."
Now in a confrontational situation, I should use the word '?' Seems
backward!"

I know, so consider the difference in the two alternative ways of saying the same thing.

NOT: **You** broke your word.
SAY: **I** feel let down because it feels to me like you broke your word.
NOT: **You** are discriminating against me.
SAY: **I** feel discriminated against.

Think about it. See the difference? You are saying the same thing, but you are starting the sentence with a different word, which implies a different perspective. When you start a sentence with *you*, it usually puts the other person on the defensive. Starting the sentence with *you* makes assumptions about what the other person thought, expressed, or intended and can be very accusatory.

"So, what can I do about that?"

Start the sentence with "I feel," or "I think." No one can deny what you think or what you feel since that is what you personally think or feel. It is your perception.

"Well, yeah!"

So, you can state almost the same thing but without the implication of an accusation. Lo and behold, if what you feel and perceive based on the conversation are not what was intended, then you have not accused the person of nefarious intent. On the other hand, if what you feel and perceive based on the conversation was what was intended, you have still not accused the person, you merely stated how you interpreted the words. And even if your impression of the intent of the conversation was accurate (that it was intended to be rude), the absence of accusation does two things after it subtly calls out the speaker for bad behavior:

1. It lets the speaker call back/apologize for the rudeness, *or*
2. It clarifies the actual intent, which was never rude in the first place.

This simple choice of which pronoun to use to start the sentence keeps the lines of communications open. Try it and see.

The corollary approach to follow down the road after making the choice of these two words is then to move to speaking about *we*. That word signals collaboration. At that point, you are building a bridge of trust to set up further interactions.

And or But

A second pair of words that deserve special consideration are *and* and *but*. When you say, "I always thought you meant XXX, BUT now I know you meant YYY," you have actually negated all the words before the word *but*. If you substitute the word *and,* the sentence then becomes, "I always thought you meant XXX AND now I know you meant YYY." Much less antagonistic and objectionable. Nothing in either part of the sentence gets negated. But what if I want to say *but*? That's OK, BUT be sure you understand what you are doing and saying! Try listening for the word *but* in sentences. See if this principle is ever violated. I doubt you will find someone saying *but* to start the second half of a sentence when that person truly agrees with the first part of the sentence.

"Wait a minute!! Guess who just used the word 'but' in her sentence! Just three sentences ago!"

Very perceptive! Yes, I just got done telling you to be very careful in using the word *but*. And I was answering the question about still choosing to use the word *but*. So, what you ought to be reading into my sentence is a big caution leading into, "That's OK." It is human nature to hear, "That's OK" and think, "She said it's OK, so it must be OK." The use of the word *but* to start the next phrase in the sentence speaks volumes about what the entire sentence is striving to communicate. Maybe it really is not OK and the speaker just doesn't want to come right out and say that. The word *but* is powerful! Watch and listen for it! *However* is another word that frequently negates the phrase that has gone before.

"So following this roadmap isn't always straightforward!"

Right, and all the more reason you need the roadmap. Then you will be very clear where you are going and how to get back on the route when you have to take a detour!

With All Due Respect

The third set of words is a phrase that can be very deceptive. *With all due respect*. Believe me, when someone says those words, there is seldom any real respect being extended, either for the person or for the expressed sentiment. Watch and see if you don't agree. And don't say it yourself. If you have respect for the person, show it. If you disagree with a specific statement, say so, nicely and graciously. What the person is usually trying to say is, "I know there is a significant power differential between us, so I'm nervous about stating my position AND I still want to have my say." Just say what you wish to say. Notice I did not include the word *but* in that sentence.

Transparency and Other Power-Packed Words

One MORE word! Watch for this fourth word, *transparency*. When used in a discussion, it often translates into the implication, "Someone lied about something, kept it quiet, kept it hidden, i.e., guilt is present." When someone asks for more transparency, the implication is that whoever was the keeper of the knowledge/process did not share it. Watch and see if that is what is meant when you hear that word. And be particularly attentive and sensitive to the conversation when that word is used to describe some of your actions. It is seldom a compliment unless specifically so stated, as in "Thanks for being so transparent!" Even then, it is still a word used to contrast a time/person/sentence that previously wasn't transparent. Otherwise, why the need to point out that this statement/speech is transparent!

Here are a few more words for you. They are some of the most powerful and persuasive words in the English language: the person's name, *please, thank you,* and *because*. Other important and effective words in leadership include *advantage, benefit, value, results, investment in the future*. Also, *granite* is a hard word, although it is also a "hard" word to slip into a sentence other than when selling your house. (Sorry, I couldn't avoid the pun!)

And some words to avoid: *might* and *maybe*, as they soften the message, usually unintentionally.

Takeaways for the Wise Physician Leader

Every leader must understand the critical nature of communications. No wise doctor would give short shrift to a patient's complaint, and so will be listening to the patients' words and reading their body language. Doctors who choose not to pay careful attention will pay the price. Unfortunately, so will their patients. The exact same approaches apply in leadership situations. The Wise Physician Leader will listen carefully, read others' body language, interrupt if and as appropriate, and choose words carefully. A huge task!

Scenarios and Questions

1. You are in a meeting and one of the attendees is saying all the expected words, but through gritted teeth while turning their back to you. What is the message being sent?

2. You know the upcoming meeting is going to include a contentious conversation. Based on your assumptions of the situation, you have worked out a killer response in your head. Once at the meeting, you delivered your points beautifully, only to find out when you finished that the other person in the meeting did not bring the assumptions you anticipated, and you were way off base about your areas of disagreement. Now what can you do? How could you have avoided this situation?

3. You never interrupt others in a conversation. Can you always make your points? How well are they received? On the other hand, you may be the person who always interrupts others in a conversation. Same question, how effectively are you able to make your points? How well are they received?

4. A committee member keeps commenting about the need for transparency. What is the implication of that word? Was it a complement or an accusation?

5. A contentious situation has developed in your meeting. Clearly, the other person intended to annoy you. Otherwise, why would they have said what they did? You appropriately respond with, "You are trying to sabotage this project!" The other person reacts with surprise, either unaware or hoping to appear unaware that they were being perceived that way. How differently could the conversation have gone if you started your comment this way: "It feels to me like this project is being sabotaged"?

6. You are in a meeting and you determine, as the comments proceed, that one of the attendees is quite opposed to your point of view. Then no one says anything for a few minutes. The silence becomes uncomfortable. What are the pluses and minuses of speaking first and filling in the pregnant pause?

Resources

Bennett, J. (2015). How not to be "manterrupted" in meetings. *Time*, January 14. Time.com.

Booher, D. (2007). *The Voice of Authority: 10 Communication Strategies Every Leader Needs to Know.* New York: McGraw-Hill.

Maxwell, J.C. (2010) *Everyone Communicates, Few Connect: What the Most Effective People Do Differently.* Nashville, TN: Thomas Nelson.

Phillips, B., and Alyn, K. (2011). *How to Deal with Annoying People: What to Do When You Can't Avoid Them.* Eugene, OR: Harvest House Publishers.

Chapter FOUR
Perspective

I still remember when she came as a new patient to my office. She was in a wheelchair, filling it from side to side, and seemed quite overwhelmed physically by the chair, sinking down, slumping over, barely able to lift her head. My first thought was, "I won't be getting very well acquainted with her as she doesn't appear to be long for this world." How astoundingly wrong I was. I am usually good at reading my patients, but in this case my perspective was way off. More about this patient later.

So, by this point on this roadmap, you have learned what your natural approach is, you have learned that others may have different ways to approach issues, and you have learned about basic principles of communication. Now we are going to look at how we see things and why we see them that way. Lots of implications for leadership there!

The importance of perspective has been well understood for centuries. At the risk of beating this point into the ground, here are some of my favorite quotes on this topic.

- "It isn't events themselves that disturb people, but only their judgments about them." Epictetus
- "The question is not what you look at, but what you see." Thoreau
- Humberto Maturana explains the importance of "seeing" further with his quote, "We see the world not as it is, but as we are."

- "Every man takes his limits of his own field of vision for the limits of the world." Arthur Schopenhauer. In other words, I tend to believe that life is comprised of what happens to me!

Remember, whether or not you are the smartest person in the room, you are still not the expert on what the other person thinks and feels. Richard Rohr (2018) has said, "Each of us has our own unique imaginarium, an unconscious worldview constructed by our individual and group's experiences, symbols, archetypes and memories." I would submit that these worldviews are very real and are seldom clear to another person, no matter how smart.

Another story about perspective goes like this. The old town sheriff sat down to teach the new settlers from "back East" about life on the prairie. He related the story of a herd of wild horses that came close to their town. The young men of the town were able to catch some of the wild horses and expand their stock.

"That's great news," agreed the new settlers.

"No, it was not. My son was one of those men, and when they worked to break the horses so they could serve as more riding stock, my son was bucked off and broke his leg."

"That's bad news," agreed the new settlers.

"No, it was not. When a pack of cattle thieves approached to steal our cattle, and our young men rode off to engage the marauders, my son could not ride and was safe."

"That's good news," agreed the new settlers.

"No, it was not. Some wild-range cows came through our town and brought cowpox. Everyone in our town, including my son, caught cowpox and was very sick."

"That's bad news," agreed the new settlers, beginning to get the idea of what would come next.

"No, it was not. When the smallpox came to town with the soldiers who were on their way to the next fort, the entire town was immune because of having had cowpox."

"OK, I get it! You never know whether an event is fully good or fully bad! It depends on the perspective!"

Wise thought!

In leadership, seldom is one person's perspective reflective and representative of the entire picture. And that perspective brings different implications with it, which may also be incomplete, if not entirely wrong.

My favorite example of this point is a drawing of two people standing on opposite sides of the page in the drawing, looking at the other person. Between them on the floor is a number. To the person on the left of the drawing, the number is a "6." To the person on the right of the drawing, the number is a "9." You get it; it is the same number; it depends on which side of the drawing you are standing on as to whether it is seen as a 6 or a 9. And it is truly both. No amount of arguing will convince the other person that they are wrong, because they aren't. The best way to resolve the question of "What number is this?" is to trade places and look at that number from the perspective of what the other person is seeing. Not a bad principle to follow!

There is one other aspect of knowing yourself. You see others who have different perspectives and you make judgments about them. Guess what? Others are looking at you and bringing their different perspectives and making judgments about you! Another of my favorite quotes is from Robert Burns, "O would some power the giftie gie us, to see ourselves as others see us." Translating this from eighteenth-century phrasing to today, "O could we receive this gift of being able to see ourselves as others see us."

Not only are you making assumptions about others and their intentions, they are making assumptions about you as a leader and your intentions.

"Yikes! This leadership thing is more complicated than I thought! Who knew?"

Exactly my point, oh wise leader! You are on your way down this road!

Part of our perspective is colored by experience and by the myths, biases, heuristics, assumptions, and fallacies we have learned over time and that we bring to most every situation. Physician leaders often need to think in a more flexible manner and be able to recognize the validity of others' perspectives and, further, where those ideas came from.

"By the what?"

Ok, let's look at some other reasons about why we think what we do.

Myths and Biases, Heuristics, and Assumptions/Fallacies

Over time we have observed things, made assumptions about what we were observing, heard explanations from family and friends, read things, and gathered input from many sources, a number of which we have even forgotten about. They can cloud or clarify, confuse or explain, impair or facilitate communication. They are not necessarily wrong, just not universally applicable. The challenge comes in deciding into which category they fall. You will often find that myths, biases, heuristics, and assumptions, and fallacies are not accurate or, at best, do not fit the situation.

Let me explain the differences in these terms.

Let's start with *myths,* which are popular beliefs or traditions that have grown up around something or someone. They can easily promote direct errors in what we think and why. A myth usually results in a bias that one then brings to the table/discussion.

A *heuristic* is a little more complicated. It is defined as a method of learning, in fact, self-learning, problem solving, or discovery by experimental and especially trial-and-error methods, and is related to exploratory problem-solving techniques that utilize self-educating techniques such as the evaluation of feedback to improve performance. A shorthand for heuristic is a "rule of thumb." A heuristic can be helpful but can also be very wrong.

Marcus Aurelius put it this way regarding the third type of perspective, *assumptions.* "Today I escaped from the crush of circumstances, or better put, I threw them out, for the crush wasn't from outside me but in my own assumptions."

Assumptions are types of perspectives usually from experience or hearsay that we hang our hat on and ascribe validity to, regardless of whether applicable to the situation. Assumptions can be myths or variations thereof.

Finally, a *fallacy* is the sum of the impression we have formed based on the myth/bias and heuristic/assumption.

Let us see what some of those myths/biases, heuristics/assumptions, and fallacies look like.

Myths

The first myth/bias is the *fundamental attribution error*. A great example is a quote attributed to President John Adams: "What dust WE raise, said the fly riding on the wheel of the chariot." In other words, we see an event and attribute it to a proximate cause, which is often wrong. The events can be coincidental and not causal. For example, one statement all DOs can relate to is, "All DOs are primary care doctors so DOs can't be sub-specialists." The truth is that a higher percentage of DOs are in primary care as compared to MDs but by no means are DOs restricted to primary care specialties. How to deflect this (and any) myth? Go back to the principle of "ask questions" from the Principles of Communications, Chapter 2. Rather than accept the myth as the full and complete truth, ask questions to find out the bigger picture and the background that informs that presumed myth. Frequently, we default to the point that if two events even vaguely coexist, we leap to conclusions about causality when it might just be coincidence. That is expressed as the challenge of correlation vs. causation, a common issue in medicine as well as in leadership.

The next myth is called the *fake perspective defense*. This myth speaks to the analysis of a scenario with a setting and a resulting outcome different than would be expected, nevertheless strongly defended. A commonly cited example is of the person who is smoking a cigarette in a room with some natural gas leaking from a faulty pipe in the corner of the room. The person says, 'I've always smoked here, and yes I know there is a little gas leak, but it's never blown up before, so I'm safe to continue smoking." That statement is definitely a fake perspective.

The summary of this myth is, "What we are doing has gotten us this far and it's the best system we have," even if completely dysfunctional. That is the problem with this type of myth. Further, this fake perspective myth is sort of the opposite of the fundamental attribution error. The fundamental attribution error ascribes a connection between two items that are not connected. The fake perspective defense denies the possibility that there could be a connection between two items. How to deflect this myth? The same as above. Ask questions.

The fact that you are not dead yet doesn't prove that decisions you've made in your life shouldn't or couldn't have killed you! I am always amused when centenarians are asked the secret to their longevity. They usually cite their favorite and generally disapproved-of activity (often smoking, drinking). In truth, the first reason for their longevity is most likely related to their genes and second, to a great deal of fortunate outcomes despite, not because of, their choices!

A variation on this fake perspective defense has been labeled *the Black Swan,* a term coined by N. Taleb Nassim, author of the book by the same name. His premise is based on the example of the thinking in Western Europe where no one who was recording such things had ever seen a black swan, only white ones. All current data of the day predicted that all swans were white. Every piece of data supported that conclusion for years and years. Then someone saw a black swan in Australia and reported it back for the first time in European recorded history. Thus, the title of Nassim's book. There was absolutely no way of predicting that possibility.

We can all think of other such events in history and in medical research. In a variety of topics, we like to seek trends from the past that imply a continuation of the same trend into the future. The tricky thing about the future is that it is different from the past. Our data from the past, no matter how big a pile of data it is, may very well be entirely irrelevant. This principle applies to research data and applies to leadership. Remember, data analysis uses the rearview mirror; we are reminded that "past performance does not predict future results." Every financial analyst quotes that caveat – and for good reason. We just think it predicts and hope it will. And the more time goes by, the more we think we actually did predict it!

Biases

Now on to the topic of biases. One of my favorite authors, Wiley (Chip) Souba, MD, puts it this way: "People think they are thinking when they are simply shuffling biases" (Souba 2014).

The number and types and subtypes of biases far exceed what we can cover in this roadmap, so here are a couple of the most common.

The *overconfidence* bias has us believing we know more than we do and acting on incomplete info, intuitions/hunches. A similar bias is called *egocentrism* – we give more credit (or blame) to ourselves than others would. This is a common bias seen in physicians, as we all know. Yes, we know a lot; no, we do not know everything. Even if we think we know everything that is known about a topic, not everything IS known about the topic. New studies demonstrate that all the time, changing understanding of phenomena. This bias is even more of a problem in leadership than it is in medicine; at least we have studied medicine. Studied leadership? Not so much. And as we get older and more experienced, we overrate the accuracy of our judgments, a point well made by Malcolm Gladwell (2000).

The *failure to ask why* bias: We often ask "why not" when something turns out that we don't like; we seldom ask "why" when something turns out that we do like! So, we do not appropriately investigate the causes of good performance on the theory of, "If it ain't broke, don't fix it." The better approach is to analyze the cause of both outcomes. As leaders, we will be able to gain a better understanding if we analyze why things turn out the way they do, either positive or negative. In both medicine and leadership, we naturally default to the explanation that if some plan works, it is because of the good decisions we made. In fact, it could have been because of sheer luck! Physicians do not practice this very much, either in medicine or leadership. It is also a variation of the fact that positive studies are published much more often than negative studies.

Heuristics

Here are some common heuristics/ "rules of thumb."

The *law of small numbers* is a heuristic. It describes the tendency to extrapolate big conclusions from small samples, and underestimates how much variation can be caused simply by luck. It also encourages us to see patterns where none exist. Every physician understands this basic principle when used in assessing the validity of the published literature. Is the *n* big enough to reach statistical significance? Is the "number needed to treat" of sufficient power to validate the conclusion?

The problem is that while we clearly understand how to apply this heuristic to statistical analysis, we do not often think about the applicability of this concept to leadership and communication. Once we have had a particular leadership experience with a particular outcome, that becomes the most likely outcome expected in the future. Further, the smarter we are, the more likely we are to see patterns that do not exist. There is some relationship to the "black swan" metaphor above, exacerbated by the small numbers. Now you see the problem!

The *vividness* heuristic describes the tendency to give undue weight to particularly vivid events. The vividness of a major event affects the balance of our attention for future planning going forward. Physicians are appropriately wary of this heuristic seen in this way. When the last couple of patients with chest pain actually had a myocardial infarction with major complications, even death, that diagnosis becomes the most frequently considered cause, even when an as-yet-unerupted shingles occurrence is a possible cause. This challenge is why every physician is taught from day one to craft a differential diagnosis of all possible etiologies, in order of well-researched frequency. Not so in leadership. There is no differential diagnosis list for misunderstanding someone's perspective, so every leader needs to have an open mind about immediate past discussion/decision outcomes so as not to ascribe the next discussion to a similar outcome, without considering other possibilities.

The *availability* heuristic applies when the more we encounter something, the easier it is for us to recall it in the future. It is a variation of the vividness heuristic, just related to frequency rather than vividness. An example would be that the last five patients with chest pain actually did have an MI. Works the same in leadership situations.

The *affective* heuristic: the leader's affect or perspective about another individual in the room influences how the leader interprets the information presented by that person, as opposed to others in the room. I am not specifying this heuristic as positive or negative, as it can go both ways, depending on which way the affect leans. It encompasses and summarizes the impact of the person on the information being conveyed by that person. The lesson here is to be aware of the effect of the "affective" heuristic in judging and employing information. This plays out almost invisibly, as a comment may be seen as highly valid when it is more likely so perceived because the two conversants have known and respected each other for many years. Even if it is not an applicable comment, the receiver may accept it just based on their relationship. More on the effect and impact of relationships in Chapter 8.

Anchoring heuristic: The anchoring fact/statistic starts the discussion/assessment. This is an interesting heuristic well understood and heavily used in some business sectors. For example, in many restaurants, the highest priced item on a menu is put there specifically to set the maximum price as a high bar and a basis for comparison, with no expectation that the item will be ordered with any frequency. The $52 steak on the menu does not look as overpriced when there is a $100 steak also listed on the menu. The anchor may be way off, on purpose. This tactic is often used in negotiations; see Chapter 9.

Another use of the "anchoring" heuristic occurs when the leader makes a quick decision and then keeps adjusting data to fit. Rather than reject the initial decision choice and appear indecisive, the leader may choose to continue to justify the initial decision by choosing additional supporting data. Another name for this is the *confirmation* heuristic, searching for further information to confirm, not refute. The Wise Physician Leader gets into the habit of looking for the nonconfirming data and tries to poke holes in the data/decision and does not defer to the experts. And further, a wise leader does not defer to the extrovert in the room – see Chapter 1. The parallel in medical practice is when the referring physician receives a diagnosis from the consultant that just does not seem right. The conscientious physician asks questions, pokes holes, reassesses, and advocates for their patient. This is a good roadmap for the physician leader as well!

A couple of variations are:

- *Search-satisfying heuristic:* stop looking after finding a single problem or *answer.*
- *Conclusion momentum heuristic:* allowing current label to gather steam without considering all possibilities. Often seen when extroverts are in the room and proposing solutions.
- *Premature closure heuristic:* accepting conclusion before all facts are verified. This can be a variation of the "conclusion momentum" heuristic above.

These are all names for similar heuristics that describe different reasons or pathways for coming to a decision/conclusion, but all lead to the same thing, an inadequately and ill-conceived conclusion. Deadly in medicine, disastrous in leadership. Remember, myths and biases are not necessarily bad, and you have to recognize them for what they are!

Fallacies: What We Know That Just Ain't So

Another helpful aphorism that makes this point: "It ain't what we don't know that gives us trouble, it's what we know that ain't so." This quote has often been attributed to cowboy philosopher Will Rogers, but there is some question about whether he said it first or just often.

- *Familiar fallacy:* I repeat a statement without rechecking facts because I have repeated it numerous times and assume it must be true because no one has ever challenged me. Quote attributions often fall into this category. Does Andrew Carnegie's tombstone really say, "Here lies a man who knew how to enlist in his service better men than himself"? The internet quote sites say so. But while Carnegie expressed interest in such an epitaph, his tombstone has only the typical born/died information (Carnegie Hall 2011). The best response? Check yours and others' facts.
- *Fitting fallacy:* An error committed because it seems to make complete sense – that is, to fit into a set of other facts. The best response? See above.
- *Transpositional fallacy:* An error that occurs when I inadvertently change a fact and make it incorrect. For example, everyone knows that the song "Edelweiss" in the movie *The Sound of Music* is the national anthem of Austria (McDaniel 2020), George Washington had wooden teeth (Kirschbaum 2005), and the Great Wall of China is the only human-made object that can be seen by the astronauts orbiting the Earth (Phillips 2003). Except that all of these "facts" are transposed.

Round Rainbows

One of my favorite examples of our personal perspectives is demonstrated by a full understanding of how we see rainbows in nature. Ask anyone to describe the shape of a rainbow in nature. My guess is the answer will be an arc or a curve. Let me tell you what happened one day. I was sitting in the window seat on an airplane and looking out the window, seeing the shadow of the airplane on the cloud below. I did a double take over the fact that surrounding the airplane shadow was a rainbow, a ROUND rainbow. I did not know there was such a thing. After doing some research, I discovered that all rainbows are round, it is just that the earth gets in the way and we only see an arc. The people who most often get to see round rainbows are pilots, from the perspective of the airplane, and also people who climb mountain peaks and can look down on clouds. Also, the round rainbow may be seen when generating a spray of water from a hose at the correct angle. The components of any rainbow require (1) having the sun behind the viewer and (2) the sun shining at a 42-degree angle from the water droplets/cloud, as seen by the observer. Most of the time the Earth gets in the way, but the rainbow is always round. The round rainbow is a great object lesson pointing out the importance of perspective. This a great example of perspective and how it is affected by myth/bias/assumption, even fallacy. And it is a similar point to that of the black swan story. If you haven't seen a round rainbow, you may state with certainty that there is no such thing. Be careful as you go down that road!

Culture and Perspective

A discussion of perspective would not be complete without noting the importance of culture in influencing the perspectives of people. Certainly, this is understood when considering different age groups, ethnicities, nationalities, gender identity, economic status, home zip codes, or education. The list of possible cultural differences goes on and on. All of those differences are important and influential. However, even the culture of an organization itself is weighty. The culture of an organization is a heavy influencer in creating perspective. Culture is the manifestation of what is really valued. Culture is about messages and message management. What is valued more, honesty or being nice? Can't always do both; one will win. See Chapter 7 for Rushworth Kidder's excellent work in this area. So, understanding the culture of an organization when entering a leadership role is critical. According to management theorist Edgar Schein, culture is the shared way of thinking and feeling about problems an organization faces over time. A wise friend of mine quotes culture as "how we do things around here" (Schein and Schein 2018). A leader simply cannot function effectively without taking into consideration the culture in which the leadership will be taking place.

Attributes of culture include the fact that it is shared, pervasive, enduring, and implicit. It shapes attitudes and behavior and defines what is encouraged, discouraged, accepted, and rejected. Also, cultures can and do change over time. A strong leader will effectively change the culture by their approach, and even so, it takes time.

Another interesting observation has been made that a contentious or controversial change (and hopefully, improvement) is easier to accomplish in strong cultures than in weak ones. A strong culture enables people to feel better about what they do. The positive sense also empowers people to take more chances on change. More about this in Chapter 12 on Change.

Back to My Patient

Remember the patient I described at the beginning of this chapter? I thought she did not have long to live, based on her appearance and disabilities. Turned out, she had a simple bladder infection and responded quickly. On subsequent visits, she perked up and was quite a lively conversationalist. Over time, she started to lose weight, was able to shift from a wheelchair to a walker and one day she said, "What church do you go to?" That question startled me, as we had never discussed anything about religion. When I told her, she asked, "Would you pick me up next Sunday and take me with you?" How could I say no? She lived in an apartment not far from my church, and it was not a problem to pick her up. Her walker fit in the trunk of my car, so we started the weekly routine of taking her to church. The one challenge was that I sang in the choir and I had to arrive an hour before the service, so she had to sit in the pew and wait for me. One day when I went to her usual seat in the church after the service to take her back out to the car, she was not there. I assumed she was in the bathroom. She soon came walking around the corner and I drove her home. When I asked where she had been, she said, "I'm volunteering in the three-year-olds Sunday School class." I was astounded. After a few Sundays, she had wandered around the campus in that early hour when I was in choir practice and stumbled on the age-graded classrooms. Our routine now accommodated me taking her to the selected classroom and going back there to pick her up, where she was always surrounded by the three-year-olds showing her their treasures. She didn't have a "lap" to sit on, but that didn't seem to be a problem. She was Grandma Jane to all those little children. She had no family. She was orphaned by the death of her mother at age 3 and her disabled father's inability to take care of her at the height of the Great Depression. She was adopted by a much older single woman, who also died at an early age, leaving my patient alone at age 18. She trained in bookkeeping and made her own way. In later years, she tried to find her siblings who were also adopted out, but was never able to do so. So, my family welcomed her for all the major holidays.

One day when I picked her up to come to our house for Thanksgiving, she said, "And bring that box over there." She had attended a class at her apartment complex and had made ceramic gifts for each member of my family, which we still treasure, along with a hand-crocheted tablecloth and napkins. Over time, she also made me several hand-crocheted sweaters. How she managed to accomplish all that work is still a mystery to me. Just as she herself was a mystery to me when I first met her. My quick assessment about Jane was completely wrong. Thank goodness she came into our lives and taught me a strong lesson on perspective.

The most important point to make about perspective is, "You are not responsible for how you see the world; you are responsible for thinking that how you see the world is how the world really is."

Takeaways for the Wise Physician Leader

Our perspectives and those of the people we seek to lead are heavily influenced by myths, biases, heuristics, assumptions, and fallacies. It is not a problem to have such perceptions; it is a problem to think they are universal realities for all interested parties. Further, the culture in which we seek to lead has a significant influence on our perspectives and how we need to best approach our leadership issues.

Scenarios and Questions

1. You have brought a clear idea of a situation and a good solution to a meeting, only to find that others do not see it that way at all. Does this variance in perspectives stop the entire process? Or just alter the progress of the meeting toward achieving the desired goal? How can you move the solution forward?

2. You have come to your leadership meeting and had previously brought an assumption/myth/bias to a conversation that was later proved wrong. You expected pushback but it never materialized. You misread what other attendees thought. The opposite situation also occurs at that very same meeting, where another person had an incorrect assumption/

myth/bias that impaired the progress in a meeting. How can you address that situation? How can you "inoculate" yourself against your own myths/biases?

3. The last three meetings have resulted in a decision to increase the price of a service provided by the organization. A similar discussion is again on the table. The availability heuristic (rule of thumb) is leading the group to make a similar decision. How can the leader use this new awareness of heuristics to identify this specific heuristic, clarifying its impact on the decision-making process?

4. Have you ever seen a round rainbow?

Resources

Carnegie Hall. (2011). Here lies a man who knew how to enlist in his service better men than himself. Carnegie Hall. www.carnegiehall.org/Blog/2011/08/Here-Lies-a-Man-Who-Knew-How-to-Enlist-in-His-Service-Better-Men-Than-Himself.

Gladwell, M. (2000). *The Tipping Point*. New York: Little Brown.

Goleman, D., Boyatzis, R., and McKee, A. (2004). *Primal Leadership*. Boston: Harvard Business School Press.

Kirschbaum, J. (2005). George Washington's false teeth not wooden, NBC News, January 27, https://www.nbcnews.com/id/wbna6875436.

McDaniel, S. (2020). No, "Edelweiss" is not an Austrian folk song or a Nazi song. Tales of Time Forgotten, May 12, https://talesoftimesforgotten.com/2020/05/12/no-edelweiss-is-not-an-austrian-folk-song-or-a-nazi-song/.

Phillips, T. (2003). Space station astrophotography. NASA Science, March 24, https://science.nasa.gov/science-news/science-at-nasa/2003/24mar_noseprints/.

Prince, D. W. (2000). *Communicating Across Cultures*. Greensboro, NC: Center for Creative Leadership.

Rohr, R. (2018). Imagination. Center for Action and Contemplation, May 14, cac.org.

Schein, E. H., and Schein, P. (2018). *Humble Leadership: The Power of Relationships, Openness, and Trust*. Oakland, CA: Berrett-Koehler Publishers.

Souba, W. (2014). *Innovative Leadership Workbook for Physician Leaders*. Tucson, AZ: Integral Publishers.

Chapter FIVE
Decision–Making That Works

Steven Covey said, "I am not a product of my circumstances; I am a product of my decisions" (Covey 1989). Thank you, Mr. Covey, for stating this so clearly because I agree completely. I am not limited and buffeted by my circumstances; I get to make my own decisions, which then set my course.

Much of leadership is about making decisions or problem solving. The way I look at it, these are two sides of the same coin. Problem solving and making decisions both require analysis of the situation, proposing different options, considering the advantages and disadvantages of the options, and choosing the best one. For purposes of this discussion, we will present "problem solving" in the context of decision-making.

Often, the tasks ahead look extremely daunting. Much to be done and a very short time to accomplish the task. Just remember, "once begun is half-done."

"How can that be? This task of learning how to be a physician leader looks like it is going to take a LONG time!"

The point? Get started!! You won't accomplish something you never start!

A favorite Steven Covey aphorism is, "Start with the end in mind." This applies especially to the principle of "being prepared." What do you want to accomplish? Even if you do not have a crystal-clear idea in mind, you certainly have a general direction. So, what do you need to have in place to be prepared to succeed? That's the point of this chapter.

"OK, I get the point. So how do I get prepared for decision-making?"

Devote a little time to learning the task at hand. Let's jump in with the basic approach and two tried-and-true schema.

Decision-Making Steps

We have lost one of the most well-regarded management gurus, Peter Drucker. He wrote prolifically and in a crystal-clear manner about leadership. Decision-making processes were an interest to him. His view of decision-making has evolved over time and the terminology has also evolved. With a nod to Mr. Drucker, the approach can be summarized in five major steps:

1. *Categorize the type of problem.* Which category is the best fit/type for this problem?
2. *Define the problem.* What problem are we trying to solve?
3. *Set goals.* What will limit the ideal dreams to the more realistic goals?
4. *Make an action plan.* How will we stay on top of the implementation?
5. *Get feedback.* What went well, and what didn't?

Categorize the Type of Problem

What kind of problem are you facing?

- Generic problem
- Unique problem (you have never encountered before)

- Truly unique problem (never encountered in the history of the world)
- Appears unique that is really generic

This categorization exercise promotes better analysis of the problem. If the problem is unique, then a previously analyzed problem will likely not offer insights. If the problem is generic or appears unique but is really generic, the Wise Physician Leader can guide through previous processes that led to the solutions. The challenge is to clearly categorize. Mis-categorization leads in the wrong direction and wastes time and energy.

Define the Problem

Albert Einstein is famous for saying if he had an hour to make a decision, he would spend 59 minutes defining the problem and 1 minute actually making the decision. That is an oversimplification, but he makes an important point. All consequences cannot be explored, and every decision has unanticipated ones, so the process must include identification and analysis of as many factors as can be identified.

This is the time you ask the questions, probe the situation, dig deep for underlying factors.

Set Goals

The process of creating goals must be conducted prior to assessing decisions. If the finances are finite (and where is that not the case?), then it keeps the discussion of options within limits if those parameters have already been discussed.

Further questions to assess can be: are there competing interests for those resources, who are the supporters/opponents and how much power/influence do they each wield?

Another question, what additional data would you need that might lead you to make a different decision than what may be obvious at first look?

And the parameters can change not only during the decision-making process but during the implementation phase. The goals may even change.

The point is to keep that in mind and be flexible to alter processes and plans as needed. It doesn't mean the process has failed; it means the process is real. See the distinction between process and content with analysis below.

It is also important to remember, that looking for ways to "expand the pie" is also part of the analysis process. So, while setting goals is a critical part of the process of decision-making, one must not discount solutions/options that may contain components that can reset/expand the parameters.

Make an Action Plan

This may seem like the easy part but is often where decision-making stumbles. What are the steps? Who is in charge of each step? What is the reporting timeline? What are the metrics for each step? Who are the people on the team who are responsible for each step of the action plan? Sometimes it feels that when this step is complete, the job is done. Not so!

For one thing, as the action plan is carried out, additional issues must often be negotiated. That brings up a two-part question: What is the best decision, and what is the BATNA (best alternative to a negotiated agreement)? We'll get into greater depth about BATNA in Chapter 9. But for now, it is important to understand that the option that best meets our goals might not be fully feasible in its ideal form. So the wise leader carefully analyzes the best alternative option/s.

Get Feedback

This step is often overlooked. When the decision is fully implemented, what worked well, and why, and what other issues were encountered? What adjustments had to be made in the plan? Completing this step well will facilitate further decision-making tasks.

Part of feedback involves reflecting on the process and ultimate decision. In retrospect, a decision that did not turn out to be optimal may trigger the reflective question, "What were you thinking?" The corollary question that should also be asked is, "What WEREN'T you thinking?" Think about it!

Process and Content

I mentioned this concept earlier. The process is not the means to an end. The process is the goal. This discussion fits into Step 4.

"The process is the goal? Isn't the process, the process? And the goal, the goal?"

Astute observation! Stick with this part of the roadmap a little longer and it will become clearer.

I think this idea of process and content is a very handy concept that a lot of leaders miss and thus are more prone to repeat mistakes. Or use ineffective and inappropriate approaches. The default of most leaders is toward content. It usually goes like this: We are discussing an issue scheduled to come before an upcoming meeting. We analyze the parameters and make a decision. The next time a similar content issue comes up, we reflect on the earlier decision, making a similar one. That is very likely to be a mistake.

Leadership is very much about process AND content, as is much of learning. You need to learn the process and all its steps before you can apply those steps to the situation at hand. Nowhere is this more clearly demonstrated than in learning medicine. Every medical school teaches physical examination skills, history-taking skills, an orderly approach to the patient encounter, how to write a SOAP note, and many more steps before the student is unleashed on the real patient. This represents the "process." They also learn "content," but only in the context of the process.

The extreme importance of process is emphasized in the patient–actor live scenario testing approach of the Objective Structured Clinical Examination (OSCE). The student who leaps to the correct diagnosis without proceeding through the appropriate steps will fail that patient encounter examination. In contrast, the student who follows all the steps in the history-taking, physical exam, assessment, development of the differential diagnosis, selecting the most likely options and developing the plan, yet lands off the mark, but having followed the correct procedure, will pass. The process is the key. The content of the topic will be learned, but skipping steps in the process can unalterably obscure the correct diagnosis and damage patients.

Another story: The new department chair came from outside the system. The chair–mentor assigned to provide orientation to the organization carefully laid out an orientation plan and a list of all-important aspects of the chair position in order of importance. After three months, the new chair was fitting comfortably into the new position. When the next new department chair was selected who happened to be an internal candidate, the same chair–mentor was assigned to provide orientation, as the previous experience had gone so well. In contrast to the assessment outcome of the earlier appointed chair, at the assessment session in three months, the newest chair had made many more mistakes. The dean talked to the new chair and discussed parameters of the position. It became clear that the new chair was not briefed on several of the required tasks. The dean met with the chair–mentor, who had worked with both new chairs and inquired as to her opinion about the orientation process. After detailed discussion, it came to light that she had not followed the same process for chair #2 (internal) as for chair #1 (external). She had made some assumptions about what the internal chair already knew, while understanding that the external chair could not have possibly known those processes. The real problem was the chair–mentor did not approach the orientations as a uniform process with different content. Some steps for chair #2 did indeed need to be skipped but needed to be assessed first. Follow the process!

Another story. The villagers had small huts as homes and kept their animals in the same enclosures. One day a hut caught fire. The family got out alive, but the hut was burnt to the ground as well as their animal, a calf. Soon the villagers started to detect a delicious smell, roast beef. They dined and enjoyed the meal. In about a week, the villagers decided another such meal would be appreciated. So, what did they do? They burned down another hut!! They understood and enjoyed the content; they just did not understand the process required to obtain that content. But don't be so quick to laugh at their ignorance. As leaders, we do this more often than we would like to admit. We tackle a problem and manage to solve it. We congratulate ourselves but pay no attention to the process that got us there. Then we tackle the next problem as though we had never solved a problem before! So, enjoy the roast beef!

Decision–Making Process Structure

What is the best way to set up the process? One of the simplest approaches is to set up a 2 × 2 matrix, as shown here.

	Positive Outcome	Negative Outcome
Implement Option		
Do Not Implement Option		

Figure 5.1   Process Structure.

If you implement the decision under consideration, what are (a) the positives that may result and (b) the negatives that may result?

If you do not implement the decision under consideration, what are (a) the positives that may result and (b) the negatives that may result?

I have found that in a decision-making setting with your team, it assists the visualization of the process to put the 2 × 2 matrix on a whiteboard in plain sight. It is important to fill in all four quadrants in the grid. It quickly becomes apparent that the positive side of the change action on one corner often has the same points as the negative side of staying the course on the opposite corner. That aspect of checks and balances ensures that the points being considered are fully thought out.

There is a further advantage of using the visual 2 × 2 grid. It stops the rush to judgment that can grab a group when a great idea is proposed. Or a mediocre idea by a forceful extrovert who has a fast "first gear," as many extroverts do. See Chapter 1, Know Yourself. Forcing the exercise to analyze even just the basic four quadrants of the grid makes it very clear that every idea has a downside, and staying the course is not always a bad idea. The unspoken point is that if one of the four quadrants of the grid is empty, the analysis is not yet done. Every option must be considered separately and analyzed individually.

> *"OK! Now I have done the analysis of a set of options. So, can I just use the next fully analyzed option in the future, based on its content? It worked, didn't it? Don't make this harder than it needs to be!"*

A good and thoughtful question. I wish it were that easy. The point is that the milieu changes, people change, and stakes change, so just defaulting to a similar choice based on the previous analysis of a similar circumstance is not the best approach. It is certainly possible that you may come to the same decision regarding the same content. But you will have affirmed that the circumstances are still the same, and it is again the best decision. Peter Drucker, that famous management guru we met at the beginning of this chapter, has said that when you accomplish the first item on your priorities to-do list, you must not go to the second item, but you ought to reassess the priorities to be sure you are pursuing the next most important issue. We will get to the issue of priorities and goals later, but the same principle applies there. Bottom line, a content-based decision that was the right one in view of the circumstances at the time may not be the right one in view of the circumstances now. Follow the process/roadmap!

Searching for alternatives and then choosing the first one that comes to mind, instead of doing a good and thorough evaluation, can lead you down the wrong path. Don't take this shortcut – follow the roadmap!

How I Used This Analysis Approach to Make a Major Life Decision

One of the most challenging decisions I have ever made was to leave practice and become a dean. In the MD world, someone being considered for a position as dean would most likely be coming from the full-time academic world, usually from an assistant or associate dean position – certainly, from the ranks of currently employed faculty either at that institution or another similar one. The safety net in case the move to being dean does not work out is the presence of a practice-based position, so that if even the previously held intermediate dean level position had been filled, there would always be patients to care for in the university's hospital system – thus, a position for the past-dean to occupy. This is less likely in the DO world.

Many COMs run much leaner, so that while a dean might come from the practice ranks in a university clinic setting, another physician would immediately be engaged to provide care for those patients. Thus the "space" to which the dean could return would be filled. Seldom have I seen a DO dean leave that position and return to university-employed practice, especially in the same institution. That option appears to be less common. So, when considering leaving my private practice, I was faced with a significantly high-stakes decision. The position of dean I was considering was not even in the same state. And there was no practice position at the university for me to fill as a physician in order to keep my clinical skills sharp, even on a part-time basis, let alone to return to, if I didn't work out or like being the dean. Further, my current medical practice with three physicians would need to engage another physician to manage the patient load. So, after a fairly short period of time, returning to my current practice would not be an option, either. The image of the burning bridge came to mind.

Thus, the need for some major decision-making analysis to be as sure about this decision as possible. So, I set up an analysis grid to detail the options.

Positives of staying in practice:
- Established practice with a good income due to a current patient base that continued to grow; a great deal of stability.
- Doing something at which I am very skilled and well regarded – no arrogance there!
- Able to teach students/residents one on one, something I love to do!
- In charge of my own practice and all my own practice decisions.
- Have two great physician colleagues whom I call my "other two husbands," as we often spent more time together than I did with my husband. They are two of the best physicians I have ever worked with.
- Arizona! I am near family and friends and church.

Negatives of staying in practice:
- Not as challenging as it once was, after 17 years in the same setting.
- Fewer new learning opportunities for a practice-based physician due the above point.
- Restricted time-out-of-office for organized medicine meetings that generate no income, while the expenses continue.

Positives of becoming dean:
- Great learning opportunity. Little did I know! Or appreciate the difference between opportunity and requirement!
- Opportunity to enter an entirely new world of medical experiences, the academic world.
- Opportunity to teach classes of students, having an impact on hundreds of students, not just one at a time.
- The chance to guide the educational focus through the curriculum for further generations of osteopathic physicians to be all they can be, for themselves and for their patients; to make a difference of greater impact and thus greater significance than being in a private practice.
- More flexibility to be out of office for organized medicine meetings once I learned the ropes, because of a team of administrators.
- This position is at one of if not THE premier COM in the nation.
- Chicago has cold weather, but with the great flight connections, I could be in Arizona in three hours.

Negatives of becoming dean:
- I was never engaged in full-time academics so that lexicon was still fairly unfamiliar to me.
- The dean position was in an institution where I knew almost no one. I did not know the culture, or even appreciate how important that is in an institution.
- Chicago has cold weather! Did I mention that already?
- The position would necessitate a move from AZ to IL, which was a nonstarter for my husband.
- Would not have one-on-one student educational experiences, but with groups of students. And when that interaction is one-on-one, as dean that is often not a pleasant experience for either party. Could I be tough enough to make the right decisions?
- For the first time in 25 years, I would not be self-employed; could I adjust to answering to a boss?
- What if I did not like being dean? Or could not make it work? Then what would I do? I fully understood that being out of private practice for even a few months would render me out of date and unable to practice. The other consideration was that each of these points was important, but not equally so. The downside of living in a four-seasons climate with very cold weather was not as much of a deterrent as having the opportunity to learn new things was an incentive. I will discuss that consideration in more detail later.

I worked on this list for a couple of weeks. I knew that I had to make a decision soon, or the opportunity would be offered to someone else. Every COM has to have a dean, even if only on an interim (very short term) basis. And it was not like there were dean positions open every time you turned around. At the time, there were only 21 COMs in the United States, so there were very few positions open at any particular time. So, while not a once-in-a-lifetime opportunity, it might be years before another dean position in which I would be interested might open up. And not all COMs were in such great shape. And how do you find that out? That is information that the COM is not eager to have made public. Not all COMs were that easy to get to from AZ. This was especially important because my husband said, "I know you would like to be a dean. Drop in when you are in town." He was not going to move from Arizona, and I did not want to sell our dream home, which we had just built four years before.

You know what happened. I stepped away from private practice. And I never looked back. Third best decision of my life.

#1 – marrying my husband
#2 – becoming a doctor
#3 – becoming a dean

I followed this aphorism attributed to W. J. Slim as well: "When you cannot make up your mind which of two evenly balanced courses of action you should take – choose the bolder," I would counter that most courses of action are not evenly balanced, but the recommendation to be bold is a good one. To make this leap to be dean was definitely the bolder choice.

Another popular quote that applies: "When all is said and done, you will regret the things you didn't do more than the ones you did." I did give that some thought when deciding to bungy-jump in New Zealand, but that's another story! The safe choice? Stay in practice. The bold choice? Take the dean job. The choice I chose not to regret, by giving it a chance? Becoming dean.

Decision Analysis Matrix

Now we are going to look at an approach that does not directly compare different options to each other, but it makes the analysis very focused on each individual option set, in isolation. One option analysis per line. Then the analysis of each option can be compared to all the analysis of the other options. For the purpose of comparing multiple factors of multiple options, a *decision analysis matrix* such as that by Pugh is better suited to the process described in Step 4 (Pugh 1981). This approach starts with identifying the factors that you will consider in making your decision. For purposes of this explanation, let's say you are considering purchasing a new piece of software. Factors to consider might be initial cost, annual subscription and maintenance fees, accommodations that might need to be made in current software processes, and ease of learning the new software.

Factors	Cost	Quality	Difficulty in Imple-mentation	Educa-tional Value	Amenable Faculty	Total Score
Weights						
Option 1						
Option 2						
Option 3						
Option 4						

Figure 5.2   Decision Analysis Matrix – Step One.

Then rate the significance of each of these factors, on a scale of 1–5, with 5 indicating this factor is of primary significance in assessing the options. If you have highly computer-literate team members, the ease of learning new software may not be a highly significant consideration and therefore will be a lightly weighted factor, as opposed to having a very large team that has members who are quite computer-challenged. If all factors are equally highly important, then each factor would rate a 5.

After determining the significance of each factor, then rate each of the options in each of the predetermined factors. Again, use the 1–5 scale, with 5 being the best of the options for that factor. If all options cost the same, then all options could be rated the same for the cost factor. For purposes of this simple type of analysis, in the assessment of cost, the lowest cost item

Factors	Cost	Quality	Difficulty in Imple-mentation	Educa-tional Value	Amenable Faculty	Total Score
Weights	4	5	3	5	2	
Option 1						
Option 2						
Option 3						
Option 4						

Figure 5.3   Decision Analysis Matrix – Step Two.

Factors	Cost	Quality	Difficulty in Imple-mentation	Educa-tional Value	Amenable Faculty	Total Score
Weights	4	5	3	5	2	
Option 1	5	3	5	4	5	
Option 2	2	3	4	5	4	
Option 3						
Option 4						

Figure 5.4   Decision Analysis Matrix – Step Three.

would be rated a 5, while the highest cost item would be rated a 1. This analysis matrix requires that the "good" ranking gets the higher number.

Now multiply all the factor weightings by the option rankings within each option. The highest score would be expected to be the most desirable option. Such analysis cannot be followed blindly, as the entire assessment must still pass the sniff test. If it doesn't smell right, it's not. In that situation, it may be necessary to reassess factors. Maybe there are other factors or sub-factors that did not become apparent at first. And these factors needed to be added to the analysis grid. Or the rankings may have been influenced by other external points that were not readily apparent at first.

Not every decision will need this type of analysis, but now you know how to do it, if needed. As you saw I used the 2 × 2 matrix analysis schema

Factors	Cost	Quality	Difficulty in Imple-mentation	Educa-tional Value	Amenable Faculty	Total Score
Weights	4	5	3	5	2	
Option 1	5 = 20	3 = 15	5 = 15	4 = 20	5 = 10	80
Option 2	2 = 8	3 = 15	4 = 12	5 = 25	4 = 8	68
Option 3						
Option 4						

Figure 5.5   Decision Analysis Matrix – Step Four.

when trying to decide between staying in practice or leaving practice to become dean. The ratings-based matrix schema did not turn out to be as helpful an approach as so much of my analysis was fully subjective, not easily lending itself to being reduced to a numerical assessment. However, remember a subjective rating approach is no less important and impactful than a numerically based rating. Trust your gut! There is no easy approach to this type of analysis.

Burn Rate

Another helpful consideration for analysis is *burn rate*. In other words, how much work goes into each dollar earned, and is the effort worth it? I remember a plan we were working on for an organization's fund raiser for a worthy project. We sold chances to win one of three prizes, a donated vehicle and two cash prizes. Let's just say our working group was highly enthusiastic in its assumption of the number of sales that could be generated, and not so enthusiastic in following through and actually making those sales. While we were able to cover the fund raiser expenses, we only sold enough tickets to cover the cost of the cash prizes, and only because one of the winners redeemed that prize over a couple of years' period of time. Thank goodness the vehicle was donated! About all we ended up raising was awareness of the project, with a lot of work by a number of people. We could have done that awareness raising with a lot less work and time. And we didn't actually raise a cent for the organization. Lesson learned!

The Problem You Dread – Or, Never Let a Crisis Go to Waste

Make every effort to welcome the very problem you dread. That is not an easy point to put into practice. Maybe that is why there are so many notable quotes attributed to about this situation.

"There is never a right time to do a difficult thing."

– John Porter

"Adversity has the effect of eliciting talents which in prosperous circumstances would have lain dormant."

– Horace

"The treasure is in the cave one most fears to enter!!"

– Anonymous

"The pie gets smaller and the table manners get worse."

– Anonymous

"When possible, make the decision now, even if the action is in the future. A reviewed decision is usually better than one reached at the last moment."

— William B. Given Jr.

These are some well-known aphorisms about the need/desirability of tackling ALL problems, not just the more pleasant ones. These quotes serve as introduction to our next topic.

The Crisis Approaches!

Some note that decision-making is much more stressful in a crisis situation. That is absolutely true; however, it is wise to look at a crisis as "something trying to happen." My favorite phrase is, "Don't let a crisis go to waste." Another perspective, "The impact of a crisis can be crippling and paralyzing or catalytic and creative, depending on the leadership confronting it"

(Burns and Dunn 2001). Another way to state this: "Crisis is a strategic inflection point."

"OK, a crisis is a good thing?"

Not really, but it creates opportunities where they may have been hard to find before.

I have found that a crisis makes people more willing to make changes. When I first became dean, I wanted to learn more about the academic process. So, I had studied the varieties of different curricula presentation models and was pretty sure I knew what would be the best one to implement. It should have been no surprise, however, that a new dean, not known to the faculty, and especially having never been a dean before, would not be accorded the privilege of immediately implementing a new curriculum of her choice. Especially since this venerable COM had a high board pass rate, excellent application numbers, and a seasoned faculty. So, I tucked my virtual "tail between my legs," and deposited that curriculum-change plan onto the back burner. Now fast-forward to the next set of board scores that came out in a few months. Guess what? The CCOM boards pass rate, which had always been one of the highest in the nation, had dropped to 2 percentage points below the mean. Unheard of!! The faculty soon requested to meet with me and asked what I wanted to put in place to turn this sad state of affairs around! Previously we had no crisis, no pressure, no need to change.

This situation created the opportunity where I now had the faculty's attention to look at an alternative curricular delivery method. We were able to make immediate changes (not a full curriculum overhaul, mind you, as there wasn't enough time) but the edits that were put in place resulted in the scores popping back into usual stellar territory. Do not forget, we must be alert to an attribution error, of course! See Chapter 4, Perspectives.

There was no way to ever know if the implemented change was the pertinent variable that generated that desired outcome. A properly conducted analysis might have identified a more likely cause for the improvement. And maybe the implemented change actually prevented an even higher bounce in the board scores! But I did not have this roadmap to make me even think of this possibility. I was simply grateful the intervention worked for the students. Also, it resulted in some street "cred" for the new dean.

Do not let a crisis go to waste! This is an important lesson for a new physician leader. There is no need to create crises, and that would not be ethical anyway. But it is important to understand the opportunity that a crisis presents. This point is not meant to imply that no change can occur without a crisis. We hope to anticipate issues and proactively deal with them. On the other hand, anticipating what might occur (and would be a crisis if it did) is another way to draw attention to and address a future crisis on the horizon, a variant of this approach. This point about the impact of a crisis is a variant of Kotter's first step in the process of creating change (Kotter 2012), presented in Chapter 12 of the roadmap.

In today's fast, changing world, what seems like a crisis may be another expression of the components of general change. There is a well-known paradigm about the types of challenges we face in life and in decision-making, which make situations feel like crises.

Our world swirls in VUCA:

- Volatility
- Uncertainty
- Complexity
- Ambiguity

The following four words in the same acronym emphasize the best approach to these challenges.

- Vision
- Understanding
- Clarity
- Agility

If the COVID-19 pandemic has taught us anything, it is that we can't control what is going to happen. Conventional wisdom has long counseled that we can control how we react to what is happening. I would submit that the Wise Physician Leader will look for ways to use what is happening, possibly even in new ways not previously considered advisable.

Takeaways for the Wise Physician Leader

Thoughtful decision-making is time-consuming, annoying, and absolutely necessary to come to the best course of action. Einstein is quoted in this chapter saying if he had an hour to solve a problem, he would spend 59 minutes analyzing the situation. That sounds like a pretty good guide to follow!

No one chooses to have to deal with a crisis, but that situation creates an opportunity for change that likely would not have been feasible in a more stable state of function.

Further, analyzing the content of a crisis issue is always important, but in many ways the process that led to the crisis outcome is even more important to analyze. This ensures that all facets are considered and evaluated. Which can then serve as a template for dealing with similar issues in the future.

Peter Drucker has outlined appropriate decision-making steps, and two good decision-analysis tools are presented. And do not forget the cost of the burn rate in implementing your decisions.

Scenarios and Questions

1. You are facing a series of high-stakes decisions that are coming at you quickly. Your group has decided to use an earlier decision, which has been retooled for a new situation without reanalysis. What are the positives and negatives of such an approach?
2. Your new leadership group is just getting acquainted with each other. There are a couple of dominant people in the group that push through a "great idea," making the point that they have been in similar situations and this was an effective approach. How well does that work for this situation? And how effective are you as the leader in allowing that approach to proceed while employing the decision-making analysis techniques advocated in this chapter?
3. At your next leadership meeting, the issue on the table is pretty high stakes, with heavy implications. Initially, people were reluctant to make a decision that "rocked the boat," even when the decision-making process indicated that was the best approach. How does the effective leader move the group to a more effective, nevertheless less familiar approach?

4. A leadership meeting had to be convened due to a crisis in the organization. Interestingly, this crisis opened up opportunities that hadn't been considered previously. How did that dynamic facilitate or limit the opportunities being considered?
5. It is human nature to consider no option other than the "best one." How can you lead the group to do a full analysis of other options?
6. Your team has faced situations of a high-stakes nature where there was a full evaluation of the situation and the best decision was made and implemented. The piece of this puzzle that was missed was the analysis of the structural pieces that led to the problem situation in the first place. Sticking to the details of the situation and outcomes is necessary. However, how could a better understanding of the process have assisted in crafting a better solution, both for that issue and going forward?

Resources

Burns, J. M., and Dunn, S. (2011). *The Three Roosevelts: Patrician Leaders Who Transformed America*. New York: Grove Press.

Covey, S. (1989). *Seven Habits of Highly Successful People*. New York: Free Press

Drucker, P. F. (2006). *The Effective Executive: The Definitive Guide to Getting the Right Things Done*. New York: HarperCollins.

Gigerenzer, G. (2014). *Risk Savvy: How to Make Good Decisions*. New York: Viking.

Heath, C., and Heath, D. (2013). *Decisive: How to Make Better Choices in Life and Work*. New York: Crown Business.

Higgins, J. W. (2005). *101 Creative Problem-Solving Techniques: The Handbook of New Ideas for Business* (Rev. ed.) Winter Park, FL: New Management Publishing.

Kotter, J. (2012). *Leading Change*. Harvard Business Review Press.

Pugh, S. (1981). Concept selection: A method that works. In Hubka, V. (ed.), *Review of Design Methodology. Proceedings International Conference on Engineering Design*, March 1981, Rome. Zürich: Heurista, pp. 497–506.

Chapter SIX

Decision–Making That Doesn't Work, and Why

So are you ready to start making decisions?

"I think I've got this down! I just learned the importance of setting up and following the process, adding in the content, and conducting a thorough analysis. We have decided on the best solution and we are ready to go. That was yesterday. Unfortunately, that anticipated grant that was going to fund this solution has fallen through and certainly things can't have changed that much. Seems like we can just use that same analysis, right?"

I wish it were that easy. We touched on this in Chapter 5: A wise person once said, "You can't step into the same river twice." The river changed, you have changed, maybe the riverbanks have changed, the point being, things do not stay the same, so reassess where you are and what needs to be done. One decision, one analysis; second decision, second analysis; follow the process! And the roadmap!

This chapter focuses on the possibility and sometimes the probability that no matter how well you analyze a decision, it doesn't always turn out

as planned, for many reasons. The previous chapter taught you how to analyze and make decisions using a couple of types of basic grids. This chapter
explains some of the most common decision-modifying principles that also
need to be taken into consideration.

First, we need to fully understand the principle of unintended
consequences.

Unintended Consequences

Every situation and every decision have unintended consequences. No matter
how hard you try to anticipate every possible side effect and consequence of a
decision, it is impossible. You still need to aim to identify as many consequences
as possible, thus the analysis matrices, but keep in mind that it is impossible, not
only to identify all possible consequences but also to assure that you understand the full implications of every decision. Because circumstances change.

Decisions have consequences.

"You just said that."

That does seem like the same thing I just said above, but there is a different twist here. Even the best of decisions made for the best of reasons
have consequences that may have different implications than anticipated.
Not necessarily unintended consequences, but the impact of even the anticipated consequences may be different than anticipated.

"What does that mean?"

OK, I know this point is about as obscure as I can make it. Let me describe
the effects of my decision to seek to serve as the president of the American
Osteopathic Association and step away from being dean of CCOM for that
year, a sabbatical as it were. It was a good decision, a well-prepared-for decision, and all plans were put in place effectively with a well-qualified, well-
prepared interim dean. I came back at the end of that year and resumed my
position as dean, having previously served as dean for eight years and subsequently serving as dean for seven more years. The principle that I could not
anticipate or fully appreciate was, "You can't step into the same river twice."

Not only had some people changed in focus or even employment, but new relationships had formed, some old relationships had weakened, and some plans had become less applicable. The educational process and the various events didn't stop because I wasn't there. The institution, the faculty, and the administration made sure of that, as they were expected to do. The fact that the COM was fine, but different, was really not unanticipated, but not fully appreciated for its implications, certainly not by me.

Here is an interesting quote that summarizes some of my perspectives just discussed. When applying this quote to my examples, the word *history* refers to very recent events and circumstances. In "Does It Help to Know History?" from *The New Yorker* (2014), Adam Gopnik says, "What history actually shows is that nothing works out as planned, and that everything has unintended consequences. . . . the results are entirely uncontrollable and that we are far more likely to be made *by* history than to *make* it. . . . History, well read, is simply humility well told, in many situations." Ah yes, humility!

There is another side of the unintended consequence situation. Not all unintended consequences are bad. Or they can appear bad at first but eventually turn out to have a very good side, which was not possible to be appreciated until much later.

There are two such classic examples in the osteopathic profession. When the United States entered WWII, the DOs volunteered to serve as physicians. However, it was decided that the DO degree was not considered an acceptable qualification to serve in the military as a physician. Some certainly volunteered in the regular military; however, others who were older elected to remain stateside in their capacity as physicians. This rejection by the military was an insult to the osteopathic physicians. However, with all the allopathic physicians who enlisted having left their patients in order to care for the military, the DOs were left to care for a new segment of the American public who had not known of their existence. A friend of mine mentioned recently that he was delivered by a DO in 1942. His mother told him, in later years, that the DO in town was the only available physician providing OB care in their area, an unintended consequence that ultimately spread the word about osteopathic medicine.

The second example was a result of the decision of the California Osteopathic Association (COA) to merge with the California Medical Association, which ultimately occurred in 1962. The details of this decision have been outlined in a couple of books. This merger led to the granting of a degree by the state of California for the fee of $62 for any DO licensed in California who wished to relinquish their DO degree and apply for what was sometimes referred to as the "little md" degree. The majority of the state's DOs did so. In the big picture, such a decision was mandated for any DO on staff at a California hospital if they wished to maintain hospital privileges. The American Osteopathic Association (AOA) was very upset by the decision of the COA. The AOA House of Delegates voted to rescind the charter of the COA. The impact of this decision cannot be minimized, as California was the largest state society in the AOA, comprising nearly 20 percent of the entire AOA membership. It was a dark day for the profession as a whole, and certainly for the AOA. The conventional thought was that other states would likely follow suit and the AOA would fade away and there would be no more DOs, each having received an "md" degree granted by their state. That did not happen; COA was the only state society that ultimately merged with its MD counterpart. However, the unintended consequence was that in 1963, the US Civil Service Commission, citing the events that happened in California as outlined above, announced that for its purposes, the DO and the MD degree were equivalent degrees for the practice of medicine, the first US governmental agency to make such a determination − another amazing and very positive unintended consequence. A follow-up note: the AOA chartered a new and very successful osteopathic organization in California, the Osteopathic Physicians and Surgeons of California.

There are many challenges to doing decision-making well. One of the first things to consider is what assumptions we make about making decisions. I know we already discussed assumptions in Chapter 4, but these assumptions are specifically related to making decisions, and not just the general assumptions and perspectives.

Here are nine factors to be taken into consideration in the decision-making process as we approach this fork in the road.

Sunk Costs

Here is an example of how this assumption works. We needed to update the state association's membership record-keeping program. One of the association's employees was assigned to start working on the project and obtained approval to purchase a new software program, installed it, and input a significant portion of the database. That employee left several months ago, and now the association has a new, trained employee who is now ready to tackle this new program. The problem is that now there is a new, more complete, and more desirable program, but it is not adaptable/compatible with the system already started, let alone can process the data already entered at a significant cost to the organization. Either we abandon the older program, the cost of which is not refundable, or we try to make it work as best as possible and not lose the investment already made. That original investment is called *sunk costs,* or the amount of money already spent that cannot be recouped. Instead of looking at what is the best function for the association, we get caught up in concern for the potential loss of monies already spent (sunk). Frequently, the best decision is to absorb the loss and get the much better, more capable product. As a leader, you must be prepared to explain how too much attention to sunk costs can "sink" a better solution. When considering sunk costs, it is human nature to stick to a poor road where the investments are known and measurable (time and money already spent) rather than pursue the unknown (and currently unmeasurable) gains that could be attained if we take the nearest exit.

Several considerations and perspectives must be part of the analysis if applicable to the decision at hand. First, when there are financial implications at stake, and there almost always are, you have to consider whether there are sunk costs. It can be the basis of an assumption that colors the decision-making process. The basic idea is that money has been spent, the task is not complete and the item for which the money has been spent is no longer the best choice, so if the choice changes, the money spent will be lost. Do you stay with the original decision to fully utilize the money already spent, or do you move to the new and better decision and "throw away" the money already spent? It is best to apply the decision-making analysis process. See Chapter 5 on Decision-Making.

Opportunity Costs

Another assumption/perspective that people bring to decision-making is called opportunity costs, which has a couple of different permutations. The first refers to the fact that by choosing one option, you lose the opportunity to implement what the other option and the benefit from what that other option would have offered. That perspective is behind much of the discussion that occurs in the decision-making process. As individuals evaluate the opportunities, it is likely that some of the discussion will introduce and promote the opportunities of the specific choice, causing others to tout the opportunities of a different choice. The thoughtful leader will recognize that a focus on the opportunities with one choice means the rejection of all other choices not selected. This introduces anxiety about the lost benefits of the other choices. It works both ways. Choosing a less-expensive option, which also meets the same basic requirements, frees up more resources for other things. Buying the perfectly acceptable $700 piece of hardware, rather than the $1000 one, leaves $300 to buy more software.

Infraction Inertia

A further aspect of the opportunities cost perspective recognizes that the more opportunities that are presented, the less satisfaction of choosing one of those opportunities. Having so many opportunities can cause *infraction inertia,* which means that in order to avoid regret, individuals won't choose anything at all. In other words, with lots of choices, which you cannot pick, each of those choices represents a regret for not being chosen. When forced to consider so many regrets, it becomes paralyzing, also described as analysis paralysis. I still remember a nonleadership issue that demonstrated this concept, where a patient of mine bemoaned that fact that having returned to the United States after a stint as a missionary in a developing country, he was now simply unable to buy toothpaste. As he saw it, there were so many choices that presented distinctions without detectable differences that he finally gave up; he just could not find a reason to buy any one brand over another. So, he didn't buy any.

Merchants selling products can get burned by this problem as well. It is a well-known sales tactic to tout not just the three major things that distinguish a product over another version, but to invent more components to try to create/demonstrate an advantage over another version of this item. As consumers, we fall into the trap of comparing the 12 added functions that a piece of electronic equipment can perform, when we only need 3 of those functions. The upside for the merchant is the sale of this more tricked-out and more expensive version. The downside is infraction inertia, such that there are so many components to compare that the consumer cannot decide which to choose and chooses neither. This is certainly not the desired outcome from the perspective of the merchant.

The leadership application of this principle is to keep the decision-making focus on the most salient points of a choice and don't spend time analyzing aspects that don't address the needs of the group. Yes, there are differences – they just don't all matter. The shrewd group member who understands this dynamic may also elect to focus on those differences that don't matter, hoping to derail a decision, using infraction inertia. Watch out as you proceed down this road!

Weak Ties and Weak Signals

Another aspect of decision-making involves the use of "weak ties." One of the important steps to take in decision-making is to be sure you bring up as many options as possible. They are not all valid for the situation, they are not all reasonable options, but there may be a nugget of value in one of them. This point is related to the one about unintended consequences but goes in a slightly different direction. The concept of "weak ties" speaks to the point that we know what we know, and we know who we know.

"Well, duh! That's it?"

Not entirely. This concept means that many of the people you know will know the same things that you know, having had similar experiences, which narrows the options that are brought to the table. A very simplistic example of this principle is exemplified in my relationship with my hair stylist. She lives in a different town and has interactions with an entire group of people I have never met. So, when I need some new ideas for specific purchases I want to make, she is a great resource, connecting me with information from people I do not know, who shop where I do not shop, and she can tap into their additional sources, which further expands my reach. The same principle applies to decision-making. Tapping the same "party of favorites" with the same experiences shared with the leader provides a narrower set of options than is desirable. Another way to state it: the more homogeneous the thinking, the narrower the range of ideas. You can head off homogeneous thinking by promoting weak ties. Weak ties are not weak because they are not important but because they are less frequently employed than your more commonly used ties.

The concept of weak ties is also related to the concept of weak signals, those small, early indications of different directions that may be emerging. With sensitivity to weak signals you are more likely to identify early evidence of emerging trends from which it is possible to deduce important changes in demography, technology, customer tastes and needs, and economic environmental regulatory and political forces. This focus gives rise to fresh perspectives and nonlinear thinking, which helps an organization imagine and plan for various plausible futures. Weak signals can be opportunities, risks, both, or just noise.

"So how do I know which is which?"

Conduct the decision-making analysis as described in Chapter 5 on decision-making!

And there is another way to describe the concept of weak signals. As I said earlier, if you bring into the conversation/decision-making arena just those people who share your experiences and perspectives, you are likely to generate a similar list of options. This speaks to the importance of diversity in all aspects of leadership. Diversity in experiences, perspectives, culture, age, educational backgrounds, race, gender, on and on. The evidence is very strong that increased diversity leads to higher-quality decision-making, leadership, and outcomes. A famous quote attributed to World War II General George S. Patton summarizes this point: "No one is thinking if everyone is thinking alike." So does this anonymous quote: "None of us is as smart as all of us!"

One View Is No View

I like to tap into a guiding principle from my radiologist friends, too; one view is no view. All physicians know the value of obtaining at least two x-ray views of a part of the body. What looks like a significant shadow in one view is clearly seen as overlying vessels in another view of the same body part.

The same concept applies to leadership. Part of the decision-making process is recognizing that the first answer is often the easier and frequently wrong one. It is also, therefore, important to state the problem in different ways, which helps supplement the view and introduce more perspectives.

A favorite illustrative activity for groups to grasp this principle involves giving each group a bag each of dry spaghetti and of marshmallows. Each group is instructed to take their bag of marshmallows and bag of dry spaghetti and construct the tallest structure possible, in a specified number of minutes. The winner is always the group that constructs their structure and then stands on top of their chair or table, holding it up in the air, thus making it the tallest. Just takes thinking about a different view of the problem. Also, this principle reminds you that you can change the scope of the option, making it larger or smaller, which may change the perspective. Define problems in multiple ways and increase creativity. *Saper vedere,* translated "knowing how to see," is a quote attributed to Leonardo da Vinci. His point applies to leadership as well as art. There are some similarities to the considerations of perspective as discussed in Chapter 4, but in this context, the emphasis is not on knowing what perspectives others bring to the table, but in looking for different perspectives that no one has considered up to this point along the road to a good decision.

Critical analysis of the facts, looking at them from more than one view, is very important to the extent possible. Remember, the cat won't sit on a hot stove a second time but will also not sit on a cold one. Be sure you are asking thoughtful questions, and viewing issues from different perspectives, so you aren't just avoiding cold stoves.

Smart People See Patterns That Aren't There

Another consideration to keep in mind as you look for alternatives and options: remember, smart people will more often see patterns that are not there. They are looking for patterns, they are looking for connections. Maybe they are trying to be radiologists!! This point emphasizes the need to keep asking questions. See Chapters 2 and 3, Communication and Techniques of Communication.

It's also important to keep in mind the role that the personality types (Chapter 1) play in decision-making discussions. Presumably, everyone engaged in the usual leadership meetings is very smart, or they would not be there. So, remember, smart people with fast first gears (extroverts) may rule for a while. It is up to the leader to quiet down the extroverts and draw the introverts into the discussion. Time and again, I have seen some of the smartest and most thoughtful people in the room turn out to be the introverts who sit back and wait to be called on to contribute. It is not because they don't want to participate and engage; it is just not how they interact with the world. On the other hand, at first blush, you will likely misclassify the vocal introvert who is heavily engaged in the conversation on a topic about which they are passionate.

Doctors are smart people. Smart people like to be right. Just because everyone in the room is smart does not mean the group will arrive at consensus on what is the smart and best idea to employ. For every complex problem there is a solution that is concise, clear, simple, and wrong.

Hyper-collaboration

Juliet Funt spoke about the challenge of *hyper-collaboration* in her company, White Space (Davis 2017). She describes a situation where the leader is inclusive, open-minded, promotes camaraderie, elevates the less bold ideas, gives every idea a chance, and is nice to all. Sounds pretty good, right?

"What's the downside?"

Funt says there is a danger in giving feelings priority over evidence—"wanting to be sweet and include everybody and make them feel heard." However, people get lost in tangents, the strong personalities prevail, and the vote is nearly always guaranteed. Funt says that in true collaboration, "we want people to have some time where they can hash out the pros and cons, throw in their ideas, but then there has to be some exit strategy" where a decision is made.

What is the goal of the decision-making process? To come to the best decision possible. That requires asking questions, questioning biases and assumptions, and including those participants with differing perspectives in order to explore feasible alternatives. It has been well studied; the more diversity in a group, the better the decisions made. The leader may need to intentionally inject conflict to improve wrong-thinking decision quality as debate sharpens understanding of the options. A nicer way to put this is to serve as a devil's advocate, the same idea. If there is a room full of skeptics, wrongdoing is less likely to go unchallenged. If the options are well thought out, the challenges will only strengthen those options.

If there is little debate on a subject of importance, a strong leader will be wise to appoint pseudo – devil's advocates charged with raising counter-points. It may be necessary to look for outside unbiased experts, but it is also important and helpful not to automatically defer to them. And remember, if I say I am being nice to protect someone, that someone is usually me! Anne Wilson Schaef, in her book *Meditations for Women Who Do Too Much* (2004), writes, "I haven't been being nice.... I've been 'chicken.'" The leader must always keep the eyes on the prize – in other words, get the job done in the best way. Always go down the road that requires you to be willing to make the hard decisions.

Misaligned Incentives

Another consideration when bumping up against a recalcitrant participant in the decision-making process is the concept of misaligned incentives. It has been often said that when a person's salary depends on not implement-ing a change, the status quo will likely prevail.

Watch for this in your decision-making processes, particularly when individuals seem to be extremely reluctant to consider all options. There may be misaligned incentives underlying the situation.

Another aspect of misaligned incentives is captured in the old saying that "if things don't add up, follow the money." In other words, there may be another consideration of money in the equation, which may not be appar-ent to all those at the table, and maybe intentionally so.

There is another, more subtle influence that is a different facet of mis-aligned incentives. I must admit that I have been guilty of forcing this situ-ation. I was running a meeting with a preset time frame and the discussion had gone a bit off the rails. In this specific case, it was not because of an unrelated tangent, per se, but because of a very relevant tangent that needed to be thought through. I was guilty of allowing the meeting to rush to judg-ment without giving that tangent full consideration – mainly to be sure the meeting ended on time. That was my own personal incentive, finishing the meeting on time, which was misaligned from the accomplishing of the purpose of the meeting. As a more seasoned leader, I have learned to stop the meeting progression, ask the group to do a time-check, and decide together how to proceed. Can the meeting continue longer? If so, how much longer? Do we put this tangential item in the virtual parking lot for consideration at another time? Do we assign a small group to analyze this issue offline and bring it back? Do we rework the timeline for the project in order to give this tangential item its full due? I am not the only one whom I have seen being held hostage to a preset meeting time frame or even a project time frame and have let that time frame govern the process. This result could also be related to the hyper-collaboration point raised above. Watch for it along the road!

Another way to look at this point is that every meeting must be run with an eye to the need for flexibility and adaptability. A wise friend often says, "Go where the energy in the room is leading you." The novice leader won't feel comfortable doing this. The best leaders can do this.

"So, what if we go through the entire decision-making process, taking into consideration all these points, and still make a mistake and choose the wrong course?"

Mistakes

"Make only new mistakes," the wisest might tell us. I wish I could say all my mistakes were new ones! We are often told to fail often, but fail well. Maybe you should not strive for the "often" part but go forward with the "well" part. There is no shortage of advice on making mistakes. But here are some of my favorites.

Brenda Ueland (2014) said, "It is so conceited and timid to be ashamed of one's mistakes. Of course, they're mistakes. Go on to the next."

Abraham Lincoln, whose leadership style is analyzed in the book *Leadership in Turbulent Times* by Doris Kearns Goodwin (2018), was able to acknowledge when failed policies demanded a change in direction.

He pledged that if his opinions turned out to be wrong, he stood "ready to renounce them" (Goodwin 2018, p. 12). The frequently cited example of this approach is his eventual replacement of the very popular and highly regarded General George B. McClellan, who often failed while in charge of Union troops in the Civil War. "I began to fear he was playing false," Lincoln said (Goodwin 2018, p. 228).

Thomas Edison is famously quoted as saying, "I have not failed. I've just found 10,000 ways that won't work." (His actual quote [Dyer and Martin 1910, p. 616] is slightly less elegant.)

"Darkness, mistakes, and trials are the supreme teachers. Success really teaches you nothing; it just feels good," said Richard Rohr, Jesuit priest and founder of the Center for Action and Contemplation (Rohr 2016).

Just for balance (and humor), there is the old motto: "If at first you don't succeed, try, try again. Then quit. No sense being a damn fool about it."

Bottom line, you will employ the best principles of decision-making and still make mistakes. The worst plan is to stick with the plan because it is what we decided, and we don't want to look indecisive. More on that point in Chapter 11, Persuasion.

OK!

Takeaways for the Wise Physician Leader

Decision-making is not as simple as making decisions and then you are done. It is also about considering the circumstances that modify those decisions and the human emotions that affect how we view the world and those decisions. Sunk costs, opportunity costs, and infraction inertia impact our decisions. On the other hand, being aware of how smart people like to jump quickly to "the" answer and may fall into the trap of only seeing one view can prompt us to promote diversity in our decision-making groups. Hyper-collaboration is not frequently considered as it masquerades as agreement, but it can create a false sense of progress. Weak ties and weak signals provide additional input that is not always easily available but adds options to the situation. Finally, there are two "misses" that can be present, misaligned incentives and mistakes. Neither will derail the Wise Physician Leader.

Scenarios and Questions

1. You prepaid for a hotel room for a conference and paid a nonrefundable conference registration fee. Now you have reviewed the final meeting agenda and see that it may not be the best use of your time. How does the concept of sunk costs affect your decision about attending the meeting?
2. You have been invited to chair two different committees and do not have time to do both well. The two committees have different purposes, different groups involved, and different organizations connected. How does the consideration of opportunities cost affect your choice?
3. Same situation as #2 above, but now with three committees, how does infraction inertia affect your own decision-making analysis?
4. The meeting seems to be going well, but one participant keeps dragging his feet on making a final decision, raising inconsequential point after point. What misaligned incentives may be creating this stonewalling?
5. The presence of a strong personality with heavy organizational street "cred" and influence in a high-stakes meeting is significantly affecting the direction of the meeting. What role is hyper-collaboration playing in the flow of the meeting?
6. Not only can a crisis focus your team, but unintended consequences can actually open some future doors. How can you use these to benefit your team's analysis?
7. The meeting was called to make a final decision. The number of new issues brought up were equally discussed and considered. Then they were included in the plan as appropriate. The final plan answered everyone's requests and met no one's needs. Is this another example of hyper-collaboration? But shouldn't all requests be honored?
8. Your team has conducted its analysis of the situation. Ultimately, the team ended up choosing a less than successful option that did not go well, and that paralyzed the entire process for fear that the next option could also be a mistake. How can the full analysis process help avoid this outcome?

Resources

Davis, K. (2017). Juliet Funt: Expert in Coping in the Age of Overload, and CEO, Whitespace, GDA Podcast, Ep. 110, https://www.gdapodcast.com/podcast-episodes/ep-110-juliet-funt-expert-in-coping-with-the-age-of-overload-ceo-whitespace.

Dyer, F., and Martin, T.C. (1910). *Edison: His Life and Inventions, vol. II.* New York: Harper and Brothers Publishers.

Gladwell, M. (2007). *Blink: The Power of Thinking Without Thinking.* New York: Back Bay Books.

Goodwin, D. K. (2018). *Leadership in Turbulent Times.* New York: Simon & Schuster.

Kahneman, D. (2013). *Thinking, Fast and Slow.* New York: Farrar, Straus and Giroux.

Kopeikina, L. (2005). *Decision Making: How to Reach Perfect Clarity on Tough Decisions.* Upper Saddle River, NJ: Prentice-Hall.

Reinsch, S. (2009). *The Merger: MDs and DOs in California.* Xlibris.

Rohr, R. (2016). Order, disorder, reorder. Center for Action and Contemplation, February 23, https://cac.org/order-disorder-reorder-2016-02-23/

Schaef, A. W. (2004). *Meditations for Women Who Do Too Much.* New York: HarperCollins.

Tichy, N., and Bennis, W. (2007). *Judgment: How Winning Leaders Make Great Calls.* New York: Portfolio.

Ueland, B. (2014). *If You Want to Write: A Book about Art, Independence and Spirit* (originally published in 1938). Floyd, VA: Sublime Books.

Chapter SEVEN
Character and Ethics

This topic is the most important one in this roadmap book.

"You say that about every topic."

I know. Point being, I wouldn't have felt compelled to put together these specific topics if they weren't ALL important.

"OK, but if this is the most important chapter, why it is the seventh one in the book?"

Because if I started out with this one first, I would have proposed the following list:

"Have a good character."
"Demonstrate ethical behavior at all times."
"Always do the right thing."

I'm pretty sure the most common response would likely have been something like this:

"Yeah, yeah, tell me something I don't already know and something I can use now."

So, by writing other chapters that actually demonstrate these principles in action, we can now go back and see where these principles are applied and the effect they have.

Warren Buffett is famous for calling out his top three attributes to look for when hiring people: intelligence, energy and integrity. He lists each trait and then summarizes that integrity is the most important because "If a person doesn't have this, the other two don't matter" (Schwantes 2020). Integrity is the bedrock of being a physician. Integrity is the basis of your character, regardless of your profession. An example of how integrity is demonstrated takes a lesson from the world of golf. It's called "protecting the field," which means calling penalties on yourself and ensuring your fellow competitors and, yes, even your partners, are doing the same. This principle applies even if you are the only one who saw the broken rule. This can be a difficult proposition, because many people don't want to hurt anyone's feelings, or be perceived as being petty or unfair. Or simply don't want to have to deal with the consequences of an honest admission of error.

There is a famous scene in the movie *The Legend of Bagger Vance* where a once-stellar golfer struggling to find his game and his own soul calls a stroke on himself because his ball rolled farther after initially stopping. That stroke could cause him the match. His fellow players and even the course judge try to talk him out of it. It was after dark, and on a poorly lit part of the course. Everyone was rooting for him to succeed; no one wanted him to call the penalty. He persisted with his integrity intact. (The movie portrays a couple of famous golfers, but there is no evidence that this match occurred.) It's a great redemption story!

This well-known quote is attributed to Abraham Lincoln. "Be honest and have integrity—you can fool all the people some of the time and some of the people all the time, but you cannot fool all the people all the time." I have also come to appreciate the perspective that it is easier to follow principles of integrity 100 percent of the time, not 98.5 percent.

"What? Isn't demonstrating integrity 100 percent pretty difficult?"

Yes, I didn't say it was easy. Holding yourself to the standard of integrity means that once you figure out what to do, then you must get up the courage to do it, not the courage to talk yourself out of having to do it by saying "just this once...." My gut is always a good guide. If something doesn't "feel" right, it's not. When the "not feeling right" is pretty vague, I have to stop what I'm doing and analyze what is going on that is making this bad feeling. As Tom Peters says, "there is no such thing as a minor lapse of integrity" (Bowling 2000).

The corollary is that when people ask for advice on general points, they likely already know what to do, they just don't want to do it. Or hopefully they do want to do it; they need assistance in being sure their analysis is as complete and accurate as possible.

"Nice guys may appear to finish last, but usually they are running in a different race" (Blanchard and Peale 1988). They are running the "I will hold myself to a high standard of integrity" race.

Rushworth Kidder was one of the most eloquent and thoughtful writers about the importance of ethics and character on the leadership road (Kidder 2005). He emphasized five core values and virtues:

Responsibility
Honesty
Respect
Compassion
Fairness

He also wrote about "moral courage," and how important this is to our lives. He makes the point that moral courage isn't one of those values/virtues listed above; it is the underpinning of all of them, when it comes to being tested.

According to Kidder (2005), the three elements of moral courage are principles, danger, and endurance. It is where those three elements intersect that the moral courage kicks in.

"'Principles' I get. But 'danger'? Really?"

Yes, if there is no danger of making the wrong decision or of offending powerful people, then it doesn't take moral courage to make that particular decision. Selecting the best clothes for an important speaking engagement does take some careful thought following design principles; there is just no danger, thus no moral courage required.

"And what about 'endurance'?"

Endurance is another interesting aspect. If the decision has minimal consequences of significance, then there is likely no endurance involved, as the situation is immediately addressed and vanishes. However, if the decision has far-reaching consequences in impact and time, then much courage is required to be able to stand with the knowledge of having made this decision, as it will be reviewed over and over.

We have been recently reminded that while Congress wants to have its say on war powers, which are actually accorded to the president, Congress really doesn't want to have to vote to dis/approve those decisions. The outcome of those decisions won't be clear for what could be a long while, so it is easier to not to have taken a vote, and then be able to state in retrospect that they really were on the right side of the plan, no matter which side prevailed. If they actually took a vote, such as on the Iraq war resolution, they would have to defend the "endurance" of that decision forever. Every candidate for reelection to whatever office has had to explain a particular vote made at a moment in time. Later, more information came to light. It is often the case that the effect of the decision wasn't as hoped. All those factors comprise the endurance piece of moral courage.

Right vs. Right

Rushworth Kidder (1995) wrote that often these decisions involve more than understanding the difference between right and wrong. It is more frequently about the conflict between "right and right." He expounds on how people need to learn to decide which choices represent the "higher right."

He outlined the four dilemmas of humanity that tap into the "right vs. right" conflict. He states that every moral/ethical issue has at its heart at least one of these dilemmas.

1. Truth vs. loyalty
2. Individual vs. community
3. Short term vs. long term
4. Justice vs. mercy

Truth vs. Loyalty: Honesty/Integrity vs. Commitment/ Promise-Keeping

There are times when a commitment or a promise is made to support a particular decision of a group. Eventually, it becomes apparent that the decision didn't turn out to be the best one. But you gave your word that you would support it. You promised. Will you tell the full truth at this later date, thereby declining to fulfill your purpose, or will you be loyal and keep your promise?

Individual vs. Community: Us vs. Them

This is a more common question for physicians than it may first appear. Do you allocate resources to treat a specific patient with possible but no clear-cut benefits? And if you do so, you are diverting scarce resources with proven benefit to the larger community of patients. These questions hit social media and the popular press when a patient pushes for an experimental, not fully tested and very expensive treatment when those same dollars could have, for example, also covered scores of immunizations for an underserved community.

Short-Term vs. Long-Term: Now vs. Then and Consequences for Each

This encapsulates the daily dilemma of spending more for a treatment for a specific patient which will drop a significant cost to the bottom line of the balance sheet of the insurance company or health system for the current year, which looks bad. However, in three years' time, that treatment will result in a significant improvement and avoid a series of hospitalizations that would cost much more. It is a much harder case to make for the delayed financial gratification of a good decision than for a short-term, apparently good financial decision.

Justice vs. Mercy: Fairness/Equity vs. Love/Compassion

Another tough one! The patient's family embellished the severity of the patient's disease in order to get access to a compassionate use drug more promptly than would otherwise have been approved. So they broke the rules and must not continue to receive that drug because that wasn't fair to other deserving patients. This is a decision that supports justice. However, the patient did gain benefit from the drug, so wouldn't the compassionate thing be to let the patient continue to have the drug?

All these are right vs. right issues.

Every single one of these choices is ethical, but you can't do both simultaneously as you progress down the leadership road.

Kidder (1995) emphasizes three principles:

1. Ends are to be clarified so they will be good for all concerned to the extent that is possible and advisable.
2. Rules are principles to be followed.
3. Care for the individuals involved is based on the original and real Golden Rule, "Do unto others as you would have others do unto you," not the one that says, "He who has the gold makes the rules."

The Platinum Rule: Expressing Integrity

Helen Fisher, PhD, has invented the Platinum Rule, which says "Treat others as they would like to be treated; not as I would like to be treated." I think both aphorisms are leaning toward the same point. Her emphasis makes it clearer that how I want to be treated is not necessarily what everyone chooses. It goes back to Perspectives, Chapter 4.

Kidder (2005) points out that "expressing moral courage is not simply a trait of leadership; it is often the thing that creates leaders."

Here are five more points that demonstrate integrity in the ethical person:

1. *Set an example.* It has been said that courage is making the right decision when everyone is watching, but even more so, when no one is watching, but you. You must always strive to do the right thing. Kidder (2005) says, "What if the wrong is not the opposite of good, but the absence of good?"

"Kidder keeps rattling my chain!!"

---

2. *Keep your word.* That doesn't seem too hard. But what if circumstances change? What if the players change? What if expected resources that are required are suddenly doubled? Strive to keep your word, and if you have strong and valid reasons why you cannot, then you must explain why in a timely fashion. And this point about "keeping your word" may seem to belong to the right vs. right dilemma discussing "honesty/integrity vs commitment/promise-keeping" presented earlier in this chapter. And it does. It's not right vs. wrong, but still a good principle to live by.
3. *Be authentic.* People will follow someone who is real, more than someone who is right. Then that authenticity builds trust. Tell the truth and admit mistakes – this empowers others to do the same, and it underscores your authenticity. This is also tough. We want to be thought of as knowledgeable and wise.

"Doesn't admitting you made a mistake call into question whether you are truly knowledgeable and wise? I don't want to appear indecisive."

Not really; knowledgeable and wise people are still human and make mistakes. See Decision-Making, Chapter 6.

4. *Be consistent.* "How we do anything is how we do everything! The truth of the matter is you always know the right thing to do. The hard thing is to do it." Quoting Norman Schwarzkopf, Commander of Desert Storm. And then John D. Rockefeller's quote kicks in: "Next to doing the right thing, the most important thing is to let people know you

are doing the right thing." This is not bragging; this is demonstrating integrity.

5. *Apologize when you need to.* That is probably more often than you think.

"Yikes! Back to that 'be a human' again!"

Here are two situations that demonstrate the challenges of applying ethical principles.

An Ethics Perspective on Giving Advice

I am often asked for career advice. As I said earlier, when you are asked for advice, the person often knows what they need to do, they just don't want to do it, or they want affirmation that they are making the right decision. Harry Truman is supposed to have said, "When your kids ask you for advice, find out what they want to do and tell them to do that." A little simplistic, but it has some truth to it.

In my experience, I used to think about such a request ahead of time, figure out what that person should really do, and then in the requested future conversation, I would lay out the plan for that person. This approach seldom worked. Because it was MY plan for that person. Besides, they asked for my opinion, right? Well, how arrogant of me to think I had all the pertinent information and insight to make such a plan! So, I learned a better approach. Ask questions! Back to Chapter 3!

- Tell me about your career goal.
- If that goal isn't really clear, tell me what you really love to do.
- If the answer to that question isn't really clear, tell me what you like and don't like about your current position.
- What other options have you considered?
- What are deal breakers for these options? Some aspects of a position are seriously important, and others are just desirable, but not essential.

A question I seldom hear being asked is, "What really annoys you about your current situation?" Sometimes these are small things, but they grate and make the current situation intolerable. Can these things be brought into perspective and be managed and/or tolerated? The unknown flip side of this question? There are things, usually different ones, in the new position that will also grate/annoy, you just don't know what they might be yet.

When I took the time to ask the questions, I wasn't really getting the answers for my benefit but for theirs. My real role and best benefit to the advice seeker was to shine a light on them and what they already knew.

My best role is to stay out of the way as the expert (because I am not the expert about the advice-seeker, and that's all that really counts) and keep the advice-seeker as the focus of the inquiry.

"You have a lot of experience and have seen a lot of people in different positions. Can't you just tell them what to do?"

All that is true, but I don't know how that person views their own life. It's not my decision to make.

A Difficult Ethical Dilemma

I have also had to manage some difficult dilemmas as a dean. The following scenario is a composite of the events connected with several students. One situation occurred many years ago when a student was caught blatantly cheating. The Promotions Committee determination was for dismissal, as specified in the student policies. The student appealed the decision to me. Now let's step back a minute and put this in full perspective.

When I was early in my dean career, the approach was that the student could only appeal a Promotions Committee decision to the dean if there was new information not available to the Promotions Committee. Makes perfect sense. However, a bit of gamesmanship appeared to possibly be creeping into the process, when a faculty member was rumored to be advising students to withhold information from the Promotions Committee just so the student could have the right to appeal to the dean with "new information." I want to be very clear that I had no evidence that such advice was actually being given. Still, that didn't seem to be sending the right message on any level. So, I decided to allow appeals if the student requested it. That way, the student got a chance for a hearing one on one with the dean.

Now, whether or not that initially sent the message that the decision would likely be reversed, that was not the case, let alone the intent. Seldom was there new information to be considered. Therefore, I was not going to relitigate the situation, as I always had a very thorough, experienced and careful Promotions Committee who analyzed all the components and made fine and thoughtful decisions. My purpose was to redirect the conversation about what the student found compelling about the career plans they had focused on. What other career options would also meet their goals?

Back to the student above who appealed to me. She admitted the cheating, expressed remorse; no further information was applicable. Because she took responsibility, she was allowed to withdraw. Much as I would have liked to give her "one more chance," I couldn't do so.

"Why not? She said she was sorry; she now sees the severe conse-quences of her actions. Can't she get a second chance? Getting into CCOM is so difficult, so she is certainly smart and had to work so hard to get there."

I know, I know. And I also know there are principles that must be followed even by the smartest and hardest workers. Physicians must have integrity to be trusted to make the most ethical answers for their patients. So, as I said, I upheld the Promotions Committee decision and she agreed to withdraw.

The further point to make is, what would have been the unintended consequences of reversing the Promotions Committee? First, the Commit-tee would know it had been undermined. Why try to do a good job in the future when the dean will overturn a well-considered and appropriate deci-sion? And how can you be sure that other students didn't know about the cheating incident? And if the incident was known, it would also be known that there were no consequences for that action. I would have been saying that we don't follow the rules and we condone known cheating. No school can afford to go down that path and still state that it graduates physicians with high integrity.

The story doesn't end there. Imagine my surprise a couple of months later when she had made an appointment to meet with me again. She asked for career advice. We had the conversation described above, even more in depth this time, and she truly felt her passion was still to be a physician. So be it.

So, it was another surprise when she came to meet with me again in a couple of months and asked me to write her a letter of recommendation for her applications to other COMs. My answer was yes, if she understood I would be honest about her issues for withdrawing from CCOM. She advised me that she was already explaining her situation truthfully to COMs and was getting traction from some admissions teams because of her stellar credentials and her honest and heartfelt remorse for her actions.

Imagine my further surprise when, years later, she was a featured speaker at a conference I was attending. Following her presentation, I went up front to greet her. She wordlessly hugged me and both of us had tears in our eyes.

The Importance of Loving What You Do

I'm in my fourth career. My first career was as a medical technologist and then chief of a 60-employee lab in a 250-bed osteopathic hospital. Second, I was a physician in private practice of internal medicine for 17 years. Third, I was a dean for 16 years. Now, my fourth career is speaking, teaching, mentoring, and coaching. I summarize this fourth career as giving back and paying it forward in every good way that implies. What I have learned in my different careers is that to be successful, you have to love what you do, who you do it with, and what you do it for. I'm not talking about low-stakes, easily spoken love. What I mean is what I call "tough love." It implies and embraces doing the right thing for the right reason. It means making the hard decisions because they are the right decisions, not the easy ones. It means being honest with yourself and others. It means being transparent, vulnerable, and real. What we do is LOVE and it's a worthy task, using heart, mind, and soul. What a privilege.

Takeaways for the Wise Physician Leader

Intelligence, energy, and integrity are important virtues, as pointed out by Warren Buffett. As he also emphasizes, the first two are useless without the third. Being a person, especially a leader, requires the conviction to employ moral courage with the components of principles, danger, and endurance. The decisions to be made are seldom as easy as right and wrong but more likely right and right, with competing high value/high stakes options. Leaders must seek to lead an exemplary life keeping our word, setting an example, being authentic, and apologizing as needed. A tall order. No one said being a leader is easy. And finally, the infrequently articulated but essential component of being an effective leader is loving what you do.

Scenarios and Questions

1. The business world is full of stories of companies that ignored principles of integrity and eventually suffered the consequences. Who are examples of medical leaders who lacked integrity and got away with it? Or not?

2. As the leader, you are encountering a tough decision that requires moral courage and that also involves endurance and danger. What does moral courage look like in that situation? Or not?

3. You have met with leadership from another organization. They discussed a situation affecting both organizations and asked for your commitment to a joint decision, which you agreed to. Subsequently, more information came to light creating a conflict between choosing to tell the truth and choosing to be loyal to the agreement you made with the leader of that organization. What do you decide to do?

4. When the decision choices pit justice against mercy, what generally prevails, and why?

5. Do you always have to set an example? Can't you just be yourself sometimes?

6. You intended to keep your word. That is still possible, but has become inconvenient. Do you keep your word, which may put you in a new and difficult situation, or do you change your decision because of new information and hope the person to whom you made the earlier commitment will see the wisdom of your new choice?

7. You needed to have apologized for a mistake on your part and taken responsibility but couldn't bring yourself to do so. It was just too embarrassing. Then what resulted?

8. Can't I make an exception to this rule just this once? Who will know?

Resources

Blanchard, K., and Peale, N. (1988). *The Power of Ethical Management.* New York: Harper Collins

Bowling, J. (2000). *Grace-Full Leadership: Understanding the Heart of the Christian Leader.* Kansas City, MO: Beacon Hill Press.

Kidder, R. (1995). *How Good People Make Tough Choices: Resolving the Dilemmas of Ethical Living.* New York: Harper Collins.

Kidder, R. (2005). *Moral Courage.* New York: Harper Collins.

Brooks, D. (2015). *The Road to Character.* New York: Random House.

Brooks, D. (2019). *The Second Mountain.* New York: Random House.

Lakoff, G. (2014). *Don't Think of an Elephant: Know Your Values and Frame the Debate.* Chelsea, VT: Chelsea Green Publishing.

Sanders, T. (2002). *Love Is the Killer App: How to Win Business and Influence People.* New York: Crown Publishing Group.

Schwantes, M. (2020). Warren Buffett: Integrity is the most important attribute to hire. Ask 7 simple questions to find it. *Inc.* Newsletters, November 14.

Waterman, R. H., and Peters, T. (1982). *In Search of Excellence.* New York: HarperBusiness Essentials.

Chapter EIGHT

Relationships and Team Building

The following patient care experience demonstrated the value of relationships to me. I saw a patient who needed a specific consultation. He had an insurance plan that didn't cover physicians of that sub-specialty in our geographic area. As he had a pressing issue, I would have usually just called the sub-specialist in the area and requested that he be seen quickly. That request would have been quickly accommodated. With his different insurance plan, I had to do some research to identify the appropriately connected sub-specialist who happened to be about 30 miles away in downtown Phoenix. I did get that physician on the phone and made my standard request. I guess I wasn't surprised with the response I got: "I don't know you, I don't expect I'll ever get any more consults from you, so the answer is no, I won't work this patient into my already over-booked schedule." He was right; he never did get any more consults referred from me, especially after that response. No relationship, no trust, no consult. More on the components of a good relationship in this chapter.

Now that we are very clear about the high bar for character that must be met and is absolutely essential to be a leader (Chapter 7), let's look at how starting from that base is the launching pad for developing good relationships. And developing good relationships provides the basis for building teams down the road.

"This chapter seems redundant. Of course, we need relationships with others to accomplish anything. What is the big deal about this?"

Well yes, we need relationships, AND relationships are not always so easy to cultivate. A relationship is different than "knowing someone." I know a lot of people, but I have relationships with only a few.

"Really, as president of the AOA, didn't you meet a lot of people?"

Yes, but meeting is not the same as knowing someone, and knowing someone is not the same as having a relationship.

In this case, it is important to be sure you are the model exemplar of character and then you can effectively develop relationships.

"Really? Can't I just be friends with somebody? Just me as who I really am?"

If you aren't committed to making the tough decisions and demonstrating the character-filled life, you won't have a sound base upon which to build relationships. Believe me, people quickly take your measure and determine whether you can be trusted or don't deserve that honor.

"Rules without relationships lead to rebellion"—a good point for leaders to remember from Kevin Lehman.

John Bowling in his book *Grace-Full Leadership: Understanding the Heart of a Christian Leader* expresses this well. "One of the consequences when there is not an atmosphere of trust is that people do not speak up. They will let leaders make mistakes even when they themselves know better. Trust is at the heart of a covenantal relationship; its benefits to the leader and the led are immense" (Bowling 2011, p. 28).

"Really?"

Yes! People will let the leaders make wrong decisions even when they know better and have more information. Yes, if they don't have trust that their opinion will be considered fairly or even listened to, possibly even ridiculed.

This is also true when there is a significant power differential in a meeting or organization. There is a reason it is called "telling truth to power." A famous CEO is supposed to have said, "I respect people who tell me the truth, even when they are willing to lose their job over it!" Yikes! Thus, the issue. I have seen repeated circumstances where you could tell by the looks on the faces around the room that people would have liked to raise a counter perspective but knew it wouldn't be well received. The trust wasn't there, let alone the true relationships upon which that trust could be built.

I have also had an interesting experience in reverse with the almost total lack of relationships in a group. I was engaged to run a half-day interactive workshop with about 30 people from around the country. When I got the list of those who were signed up, I was surprised at the diversity of titles and level of positions held by the attendees. Everyone from deans to interim staffers in student services offices. I knew that if I didn't figure out a way to level the playing field, those most junior attendees would be concerned about asking questions and raising suggestions. So, I set up the workshop with the rule "first names only." Everyone was to have only their first name on their badge and was to be addressed only by their first name. Everyone had the full attendee list with credentials in their packets for future reference. This only worked because most of the people in the room didn't know each other. The outcome was that more comments and questions were able to be taken at face value than would have been the case if titles/positions were emphasized.

Find a way to say yes to at least part of the request to preserve the relationship. It demonstrates respect, that the requestors are valued and their opinion counts (refer back to Chapters 2 and 3). This emphasizes that all ideas/requests have some grain of truth and value in them. Agreeing to part of a request, or to at least consider part of the request, honors and respects the person.

Another point: Never let a problem to be solved become more important than a person to be loved, from Barbara Johnson (1996). Same idea. The problem will go away. You'll still need the relationship. Even more to the point.

The other side of that relationship coin? When people like you, you'll be surprised by what they will do for you. I became very close friends with the other deans on our campus; getting acquainted just seemed like the right thing to do. Over time, we learned that we could talk candidly to each other about our respective challenges and that information would not be fodder for further discussion with anyone else. What I didn't realize was as acquaintances we were actually falling under the category of *relationships*. When I needed a special favor or accommodation of a schedule or room availability, each of the other deans bent over backward to inconvenience themselves or their college just to help me out. As I did for each of them. I didn't abuse that courtesy by ever asking for something I didn't really need.

"What actually makes a good relationship?"

Good question! This is my personal list of how to approach having good relationships.

Approach to Building Relationships

1. *Get to know the other person,* their background experiences, and perspectives. You don't have to agree with everything that person thinks and feels.
2. *Demonstrate respect to that person.* If you respect someone, it doesn't mean you have to agree with everything they think and feel. I have friends across the political spectrum because I honor them as people with different worldviews, not as a carbon copy of my thought processes.
3. *Be trustworthy.* Trust can only be developed over time with consistent actions. See examples above.
4. *Be kind.* This point seems so simple and it is so rare. Extend yourself! What have you got to lose?

Emotional Intelligence

Now you need to consider emotional intelligence. That is critical in moving down the road in building relationships. This section describes the basic components of emotional intelligence, based primarily on Daniel Goleman's work (2001, 2005).

Self-Awareness

This point harkens back to Chapter 1, Know Yourself. The aspects of self-awareness include the following:

- *Emotional awareness.* This includes reading your own emotions and those of others.
- *Accurate self-assessment.* Seems self-explanatory, but not easy and not often demonstrated.
- *Self-confidence.* This point is not always understood in the context of emotional intelligence. Self-confidence is not arrogance and does not depend on lack of doubt in oneself or one's performance. Concern about one's skill set or one's performance is healthy, and yet self-confidence must not be prominently projected to others. Ernesto Reuben at Columbia Business School calls it *honest overconfidence.* In other words, I'm doing the best I can, I know what I know, and that knowledge builds the confidence in where I am and what I am doing.

There is another aspect of this topic of self-awareness which is not generally presented in the discussion of emotional intelligence, the concept of the *imposter syndrome,* first described in women by Clance and Imes (Clance and Imes 1978). Self-confidence as described above outlines the importance of knowing you are doing the best you can. The flip side is expressed as the imposter syndrome where doing the best you can may still not be perceived as being good enough, at least by you. The point of this aspect of emotional intelligence is to be fully self-aware, as feeling like an imposter is frequently just that, a feeling, not a reality.

I actually was an imposter as I saw it, at one time. Through a series of serendipitous steps, I was appointed interim chief of the clinical laboratory of a Phoenix hospital, supervising 60 employees when I was 22 years old. The word *interim* soon disappeared from my title and I held that position for seven years until I left to start medical school. A couple of years after starting in that position, at a meeting of all the chiefs of all the labs at all the hospitals in Phoenix, I was seated next to one of the other hospital chiefs who was nearly three times my age. I commented to him that I didn't feel qualified to be in this group, being so young and inexperienced. I had not heard of the name of what I was describing. His words were much appreciated, "You are doing a great job, don't let anyone tell you otherwise." Self-awareness!

I appreciate Arthur Ashe's admonition, "Start where you are. Use what you have. Do what you can."

Self-Management

This is where the major work really starts. The big points here are:

- Self-control
- Transparency
- Adaptability
- Initiative
- Optimism
- Achievement drive

The novice leader may lose the drive for achievement because of lack of confidence in their ability to move forward in the face of adversity. The novice leader may further stop pursuing new initiatives for the same reason.

Each of these points is generally well understood. And yet, the lack of self-management is a characteristic of the novice leader. That novice leader expresses frustration with outbursts of emotion, lacking self-control. The novice leader will fear transparency because those being led may discover the leader's lack of knowledge or insight. This same leader may refuse to adapt the previously approved plan because it requires skill and a confidence which is not possessed. The novice leader can quickly lose optimism when any aspect of the predetermined path doesn't go according to plan. This leader doesn't understand that people don't follow negative leaders, compounding leadership difficulties. Additionally, it is helpful to also strive to be passionate – this is the most convincing of the three common persuasion approaches, much more effective than using logic or the specifically and carefully chosen words. See Persuasion, Chapter Eleven.

Social Awareness

The next step on the roadmap follows the first two above.

- *Service orientation.* This is an easily understood aspect of social awareness. If we are to be truly socially aware/conscious, we will be led to be oriented to giving back through service.
- *Organizational awareness.* Same thought here; in order to be socially aware, one of the most important entities to be aware of is your organization and the bigger organization picture in which it exists.
- *Empathy.* Social awareness is frequently expressed as empathy. It is worth noting that empathy is not a basic listening skill; it is a master listening skill. Not sympathy: that is what you feel. Empathy is who you are. Sympathy says, "I'm so sorry your too-tight shoes hurt your feet." Empathy says, "My feet would hurt too, in those too-tight shoes."

I had the opportunity to talk to a woman physician who was lamenting the lack of support from her specialty organization colleagues. She was feeling isolated and marginalized. I must admit, my first reaction was to encourage her to buck up, and that she was being too sensitive. Then I reflected on how she was expressing her sadness at this situation. So, I said, "I can't imagine how hard that must be for you." It was not my place to judge her professional situation with my poor attempt at or lack of awareness. That small empathic expression was well received.

Relationship Management

Finally, we come to relationship management as the last component of emotional intelligence, and I propose this as the ultimate goal of emotional intelligence—to develop and nurture relationships, the point of this chapter. You have to have mastered the first three components of emotional intelligence in order to fully manage and maintain relationships, which then allows you to implement the following components resulting from relationship management.

- *Having influence.* The point of relationships for a leader is to have influence. Influence is most effectively accomplished through relationships, optimally positive ones.
- *Developing others.* It is a privilege as well as a responsibility to assist in developing the skill set and capabilities of others, whether subordinates or even peers.

- *Building bonds.* This is an outgrowth of relationships, one of the most joyous aspects; you don't have to be close friends, but you can fully appreciate the talents of the other person.
- *Managing conflict.* See Chapter 10.
- *Being a change catalyst.* See Chapter 12.

Team-Building Approach

I have separated out this topic to expand on the discussion.

The seventh component of relationship management in the emotional intelligence literature as summarized above is *team capabilities and collaboration.* In other words: *team building.* Building relationships with your team members creates the basis for building teams, enhancing team capabilities and collaborative efforts. It is wise to appreciate the team—likely, you are not the smartest person in the room; and even if you are, it is all the more important to engage others. Also, it is wise not to let others know that you are or think you are the smartest person in the room.

To recap, employing emotional intelligence as described above sets the stage to develop relationships, and developing relationships sets the stage for building teams. However, developing and implementing emotional intelligence doesn't happen quickly or easily. Here are some pointers for building teams.

1. *Implement all aspects of the emotional intelligence framework* as above.
2. *Conduct appropriate analysis of the situation,* no shooting from the hip or lip. This is hard for physicians because we usually must make quick decisions as we have so many patients to care for. And we can move quickly because we have the training and experience to do so. In leadership, it is very helpful to take a step back, understand there are many facets and perspectives to an issue and initially, as a leader, you don't know what you don't know. And you don't have to know everything at the first introduction to the issue. This is actually very liberating. As a leader, you need to give the best possible answer, but you will often only have a piece of the story. You don't want to give a snap answer only to find out later, with more information, that wasn't your best thought. The thoughtful leader needs to step back, ask questions, talk to more people, depend on your emotional intelligence and relationships, and get more

information and input. Besides, a snap decision often comes unsnapped at the most inopportune time!

3. *Purposefully engage in active listening.* You can't manage what you didn't hear or understand because you weren't really listening. And you can't respond accurately to a misunderstood statement. I recall a meeting where the person speaking at the microphone stated something incorrectly. He immediately corrected himself. But another attendee in the meeting who was looking to make a name for himself immediately ran to another floor microphone to correct the misstatement. Unfortunately, he was so intent on being the smart one in the room and thinking how he was going to make that clear, he didn't hear the first speaker correct himself. So when the respondent got to the microphone and made an elaborate show of correcting the first speaker, the rest of the attendees at the meeting looked at him for what he was, a sniping know-it-all who embarrassed himself attempting to look good at the expense of the first speaker. Not a good look.

4. *Genuinely care about people.* If you can't meet this requirement, you aren't cut out to be in leadership. Bottom line. Not everyone will like my choice of words, but this perspective comes from my heart, I use it, I mean it, and stand by it. I have LOVED every role I have ever had. I loved my patients, my students, and now being able to give back to our profession. See Chapter 7.

    Another aspect of this point: As a leader, it is your job to protect your colleagues from blame. That's not the same as taking the blame yourself, but the leader is always responsible for the team and the team decisions, so if there are unintended consequences, the leader must step up to accept responsibility for the team and its decisions.

5. *Show tough love.* This is the corollary of "genuinely caring about people." If you truly care about people, you will work to redirect someone making a poor decision. That doesn't mean that person will follow your advice, but you had better provide it. And tough love means not agreeing to every request when it is not the right thing to do. Tough love means following well-thought-out rules when there is no compelling, overriding, "can't be ignored" reason not to; when it would be easier to say, "OK, just this one time." Problem is, there is never "just this *one* time" and if you allow one person to avoid the rule, you set the precedent that no one must follow rules.

6. *Forgive and forget.* This is easy to say, very hard to do! (See Chapter 7 Character and Ethics). I don't even like this rule! I am willing to forgive,

but not so much to forget. What if they do "it" again? Don't I want to add that on to the previous infraction? Of course, I do! I have had to struggle with this one for a LONG time. The truth is, by *not* forgetting, otherwise known as *holding a grudge,* I'm the one being hurt. I may think I have forgiven, but if I carry that issue around with me and don't forget it, I haven't truly forgiven the other person. It has been said that the "acid" of unforgiveness burns the container in which it is carried (me). Forgive and forget! Not easy but very important to self-health.

7. *Assume the best about people.* Dale Carnegie (1936) made this point nearly a hundred years ago: give them a good reputation to live up to. The way this plays out is to assume that people truly want to do the right thing, but may not have thought it through, may not have realized there were other options, or actually may be selfish and putting self-interest first. Regardless of the reason for a specific course of action, manage it this way: "I know you always want our committee members treated equally, so I'm sure you are distributing all the materials to all members at the same time." If they were doing so, you have affirmed that. If they didn't or weren't planning to, you have not accused them of nefarious purposes. You have just given them the opportunity to say, "Sure! Just about done." Even when you know they weren't planning to follow that course of action; they now have been put on notice that is the expectation and were still not put on the defensive. And their actions are being observed and noted. If you approach it this way, how can anyone admit that they intended to treat committee members unequally? Even if the perpetrators recognize they have now been trapped into doing a good deed they didn't intend to, they are now "guided" to do so. Try it.

One other side piece about this point. *Don't listen to flattery!* I'm amazed at how many do and who those people are!

"Wait a minute, didn't you just say we must assume the best about people? How do I know if it's flattery or an honest compliment? Shouldn't I assume the best about people?"

Yes, you need to assume the best. I'm just saying that if it feels insincere, it probably is. Just an observation.

There is another side of what could be called flattery, described as *unjustified praise.* I learned a long time ago that I would get unjustified praise and unjustified blame. We all like to hear praise of our efforts, as we like to know that others recognize our work. The issue is not the praise, the issue is the word *unjustified*. That's flattery. Some will blame you in error, for whatever purpose they may have, and you can't accept that. Some will praise you in error, for whatever purpose they may have. You can't accept that, either.

8. *Be kind!* First, there is not enough kindness in the world. Second, it's usually possible to be kind with no cost. Third, even if the kindness is not reciprocated, your mother would be proud. It has been my experience that some people are rude when they can't think of anything else to say, which is not a sign of strength or moral superiority. Rumi (thirteenth-century poet) said all our decisions should be put to this test, "Is it true, is it necessary, is it kind?" Refer back to my relationship principle 3.

9. *Never hate your enemies; it affects your judgment.* There is a famous admonition: "Refuse to let past resentments fester." This is a different take on the recommendation to "forgive and forget," now taken to the next iteration and implication.

Chapter 1, Know Yourself, presented the experience I had getting acquainted with each of the CCOM department chairs. The novice physician leader/dean was taken back by the variation of approaches of each chair. I didn't understand why each person had such different emphases. I didn't understand what was wrong with them! My reaction was to respond to each of them in my usual manner: directive, authoritative, providing guidance in ways that had personally served me well in the past. Emphasis on "served ME well." I couldn't see why they were emphasizing different aspects in answers in my questions, if I even got a chance to ask them. I would say that my natural approach employs some of the basic principles of emotional intelligence, so that helped. But it only got me so far down this road.

Over time, as I have learned the lessons included in this book, I would have understood their different approaches; I would have welcomed their different emphasis; I would have brokered their different strengths. I came to embrace this understanding. On the good side, I had a natural instinct to respect people. So, I set up a retreat for these chairs. One of the most effective exercises at the retreat was to go around the room and ask each chair to describe their natural approach with a phrase of their choosing. While I would have to admit that I stumbled onto this exercise, the self-descriptions were insightful and provided significant clarity. The further surprise to me was while these chairs had worked together for some years, their self-descriptions were surprising and enlightening to each other as well. A very good start to team building!

There is an interesting downside to the idea of emotional intelligence, though. It has been said that the people who feel that they have high emotional intelligence may be more likely to be duped because of an actual overconfidence in their ability to read others. Sounds like an expression of arrogance to me—just a cautionary thought. In my opinion, it's a risk worth taking. I'd rather be duped by one than suspicious of many.

Let me tell you a story that taught me a lot about emotional intelligence. The woman had been a patient for several years. She always seemed to be a bit quiet and reserved. Over my years in practice, I came to be known as the "hugging doctor," expressing my joy at being in such a wonderful profession and having such engaging patients. This particular woman was clearly uncomfortable with this expression of affection, pulling back from my embrace, however light and tentative. I adjusted to that response and was careful not to invade her space and her privacy. So, imagine my surprise one day when I opened the door to the next room and there she stood with six sets of clothes hung around the room! It turns out I had mentioned I was going to travel to the Middle East soon and had admired an outfit she was wearing, which would be well suited to the warm climate and the demands of a two-week travel schedule. I had asked where she had purchased the outfit, as it was very lightweight and would be easily rinsed out and be dry for the next day's travels. Without telling me her plans, she went to the store where she purchased her outfit and bought one for me, as we were about the same size. She actually ended up buying six such outfits. I tried them on in the exam room, selected two, paid her for them, and she returned the other four! I never had another patient express affection in that way. She wasn't comfortable with my expression of affection, but she had a wonderful one of her own! That was a very big lesson in emotional intelligence. And she didn't have any medical complaint that day!! I certainly didn't charge her for a visit that day!

The lessons of emotional intelligence, then, parallel and reinforce the lessons of personality types. We don't have the same personality types and we don't have the same emotional intelligence perspectives. Demonstrating and employing emotional intelligence acknowledges the value of the other person and recognizes s/he may and probably will look at the situation very differently.

This point is well encapsulated in the statement, "We do not see things as they are. We see things as we are," attributed to Rabbi Shemuel Nachmani, quoted in the Talmudic tractate Berakhot (55b.). According to your personality type and what you bring to the table. A further thought on this issue, "You are not responsible for how you see the world, but you are responsible for thinking that how you see the world is how it really is." Ouch!

"You keep using this quote! I get it!"

Do you really? OK, I know I keep using this quote over and over. Because we don't like to acknowledge the truth of it! I see the world as *I* see the world. And I'm an honorable person, so what I see and interpret has to be right. Wrong! The way the world looks to you is not the same as how it looks to others. That doesn't make them wrong and me right.

"Am I not entitled to see the world as I see the world?"

Yes, you are entitled to do so, and that's not the problem. You can only see what you can see.

"So, what makes the world really 'real'?"

Well, that is also a good question. The world we see and how we interpret it probably embrace a little bit from different perspectives—individual personality types and frames of reference that lead us to see things differently.

"How do I make that work as a leader?"

Just consider that how you personally see the world situation is not exclusively and totally accurate; you just don't know which part is inaccurate and to whom.

One my earliest experiences with this concept occurred in college. The family of one of my friends in the dorm at Arizona State had moved to Arizona from Pennsylvania. Their move occurred about the same year my family moved to Arizona from Indiana. In one of those long nights of conversation that occur in dorms in college, she bemoaned the decision her family made to move to Arizona. Both of our families had made that decision for a family member's health reasons. In her case, her father had been a welder in a union shop in PA and had great pay and great benefits. The job in Arizona was not a union job, and it came with poorer working conditions and significantly less pay and benefits. The family member's health was the prime concern, so the family decision could not be reversed, but she saw the impact on her family. I was shocked. In my case, my family had traded the uncertainty of life as a dairy farmer in Indiana with the challenges of weather and prices of beans, wheat, corn, milk, and cattle for a steady job and paycheck for both parents, and employee benefits we had never ever had. Plus, my rural grade school class in Indiana had 22 students with limited educational opportunities. My grade school class in Arizona had 150+ students with every educational offering I could imagine/desire. My view of Arizona was a paradise. My friend's view of Arizona was that of a significant step down from their previous situation. We were both looking at the same Arizona. We had very different worldviews. We were both right.

Emotional Proprioception

I have invented a phrase describing an aspect of the principles of emotional intelligence. I call it *emotional proprioception*. As physicians, we understand proprioception as an important neurological property that allows the body to sense where it is in space. It is a part of the balance mechanism based in the cerebellum. I suggest that applying that concept to one's emotions makes it clear that an important part of understanding our emotions is to see them in perspective (in balance) to others and how they influence and are influenced by others.

It expresses the idea that we detect elements of emotional intelligence, and our emotional proprioception is how we process those elements to create a balanced understanding of our world.

Relationships are based on TRUST! Plain and simple. And trust takes time and attention as well as trial and error to develop. Remember, when you need a relationship, it's too late to start building one. While in my medical practice, I was part of a relatively small medical staff (180+ doctors) and we all knew each other well, as we had monthly staff dinner meetings, a hospital accreditation requirement in the day. We shared a monthly meal, some wine, and some good camaraderie, which built trust. Over time, that accreditation requirement was relaxed, and it had a number of unintended consequences (remember Chapter 6), primarily based on the loss of relationship-development opportunities—between physicians, and with physicians and hospital administration. Yes, it saved money, but many of the connections were lost or never formed in the first place. For those of us who were in the hospital every day, the doctors' dining room served the same purpose, but many doctors didn't come to the hospital that frequently, so that congregation opportunity didn't fill the gap left by fewer staff meetings.

Special Relationships You Need to Cultivate

Get a mentor, a coach, and a sponsor, at least one of each.

"What is the difference?"

They can be the same person, but likely are not.

Mentor

The *mentor* is an individual who has been in the same setting in the past and can head off misperceptions/miscommunications in this setting. It is important to watch a potential mentor to be sure they are getting the desired response from their conversations and are also open to talking with you. If the person is meeting those criteria, then it is wise to ask if s/he will serve as a mentor for you. Seldom will anyone refuse, although it does happen for a variety of reasons. It is most effective to ask your mentor after a meeting, "How did I come across? Did I get my point across?" And a further useful question is, "XX was being discussed; how did that idea/proposal seem to you? I actually read that person as really being more concerned about YY. What did you think?" That also gives you a sense of the more experienced view of a specific meeting. It can be helpful to engage an individual who attends some of the same meetings you do, even if not a mentor specifically.

Condoleezza Rice has said that mentors come in all sizes, shapes, and genders (Spain 2017). Some of my most influential mentors have been men. Mainly because there were so few women physicians when I was in medical school and residency. Some of those male mentors are still among my best friends.

I like the term *micro-mentor*. It speaks to the idea that you may have more than one mentor at a time, especially in different settings. And that mentorship can be very short or longer in duration. Seldom is one person the most appropriate mentor over the long haul and for all your situations and needs.

Coach

The *coach* is generally someone you pay to give you advice, guide you with readings, talk through scenarios. I have had two coaches who focused on different areas. The first coach was a conventionally trained executive coach who put me through a formal process. Initially, she and I met to discuss why she had been engaged in the first place. Believe me, that was a very hard conversation. I was explaining why my actions were justified and why I was not receiving full credit for what I was trying to achieve, and she started to explain where I was going wrong! That was pretty hard to hear. Not at all what I wanted or expected. We were having lunch and I literally couldn't swallow for the lump in my throat. However, she gave me some insight into why I was struggling in my position. So, I did listen to what she had to say. Then she administered some assessment tools to see my natural approaches (Chapter 1). That was followed by obtaining a set of 360-degree evaluations from superiors, peers, and subordinates. She summarized the feedback from the 12 individuals and presented it to me in gentle but firm terms. That was also hard to hear! Not all bad, but pointedly clear on where I was missing the mark.

That not so "fun" session was followed in a couple of weeks by her coming to my office and watching me work for a day. We selected a day when I was running several meetings to watch my interactions and leadership style.

She had a list of areas for improvement! I specifically recall some of her points: "You bring a stack of papers and shuffle through them during the meeting, looking for the right notes, which makes you look disorganized and nervous. It doesn't inspire confidence in your team. Summarize your papers/points on one sheet and sit quietly while others present their points, give them your full attention, and then respond." She also advised, "Don't make notes on tiny pieces of paper; they are too easily lost." And "turn off the 'ding' bell on your computer signaling a new message, as it distracts you and others." And many more. Some big points and some small ones, all helpful. The coach worked with me for about nine months, and it was well worth every minute.

The other coach was a "content" expert. That was in contrast to a "process" expert, the trained executive coach described above. The content expert had been a dean and a provost. Her approach was to listen to issues I was dealing with and to give me perspectives to consider, as well as books and articles to read about those issues. She recommended which meetings to attend, which publications to read, and which organizations to join. I talked to her monthly for about an hour at each session over a year's time. Both coaches were invaluable and served different purposes, complementary to each other.

Sponsor

The *sponsor* is yet another guide. It might be your mentor or someone else. The concept of having a sponsor is newer. The sponsor is already in the situation you are entering and will introduce you to people and the culture, promoting your acceptance, engagement and participation, and even promotions. That person will be at a higher level or will have an established reputation in this setting.

I had a sponsor when I started medical practice and didn't even realize it. I joined one of my residency mates in medical practice who had finished the residency program a year ahead of me, going to an Arizona practice also one year ahead of me. He was a very smart and well-regarded internist who had built up a strong practice following in that year. He was consulted extensively at the hospital and had a busy office practice as well. When I joined him at his invitation one year later, the situation was interesting. There were approximately 180 doctors on staff, and only 3 were women. One was a pathologist; one was an OB/GYN specialist, and one was a family doctor who never came to the hospital. It never occurred to me that I was breaking into a male bastion of medical practice, where I would be the first woman who presented herself to be called in optionally for consultations by the male doctors for general hospital admissions.

My partner/sponsor managed this situation beautifully. He immediately announced to all the referring doctors that no matter which of us they ordered to perform the consultation in the hospital, the two of us would take all the consultations on an alternating schedule, switching back and forth every other night and every other weekend. He was very busy and needed to get some sleep, too! So immediately, I was bestowed with the imprimatur of his quality of work, and the referring doctors had the opportunity to see the quality of my work, too. I still remember a family doctor who had referred a patient who needed a colonoscopy. He just "happened" to be available to watch me do this first procedure, and after he saw how skillfully I was able to perform the scoping, he never seemed to be available to sit in again. Although my partner and I didn't plan for a sponsorship relationship, that is exactly what happened and smoothed the way to a successful hospital-based practice for me. And I was elected chair of the Internal Medicine Department in a couple of years, then chief of staff (for two terms!) in a couple more years! Sponsorship is VERY important!

When entering a new situation, it is wise to identify a sponsor who is well regarded, who knows you and who is willing to take you under her/ his wing to introduce you and guide you in this new arena. It is a very different role than mentor or coach and is very important. Just be very careful that your sponsor has appropriate status and is willing to honestly serve in this role for you.

The next step in the role model, mentor, sponsor sequence/continuum is to become one yourself for others. Pay it forward!

Remember, because of relationships and their ultimate effectiveness in facilitating team building and ultimately the desired accomplishments, bet on people, not strategies. Contentment is found in relationships, not nearly as much as in accomplishments. Relationships are our most powerful and reliable 401(k), according to Richard Rohr (2019).

Takeaways for the Wise Physician Leader

Studying, learning, and experience are how you acquire knowledge of what to do. Relationships are the key to how you employ that knowledge to do what you do. And the key to relationship building is to employ emotional intelligence. You can have the best ideas and plans but if you have annoyed everyone who must implement those ideas and plans, good luck in getting things accomplished. The further use of these principles of developing good relationships is that these same principles apply to building teams, the structure that facilitates needed accomplishments. The Wise Physician Leader understands that employing the original and honorable Golden Rule is a great start on learning principles of emotional intelligence.

Scenarios and Questions

1. After a team, of which you are a member, has managed a particularly contentious issue, you find out the leader has been talking about the team and its decision to other groups in less than glowing terms. How likely is his team to have open and honest conversations at their next meeting?
2. The dean calls you into her office to review a specific issue in the department that you chair. In the course of the conversation, she asks for your assessment of your fellow chairs and their effectiveness in their departments. What are the positives and negatives of such a discussion?
3. You watch as a novice leader clearly tramples on the principles of emotional intelligence, leaving them in shambles. How successful was she in accomplishing her goals?
4. Physicians work quickly. Why can't leaders just do the same? We're smart!?
5. Isn't it just easier to say yes as a leader? Then won't everyone appreciate and like you? Why or why not?
6. Dale Carnegie (1936) says to give people a good reputation to live up to. Shouldn't people take responsibility for their actions and get called out for actual and bad action as appropriate? Toughen up! How well have you seen that approach work?
7. Describe situations where it was or would have been helpful to have a mentor, coach, or sponsor. What were the downsides?

Resources

Bolton, R. (1979). *People Skills: How to Listen to Others and Resolve Conflicts.* New York: Touchstone.

Bowling, J. (2011). *Grace-Full Leadership: Understanding the Heart of a Christian Leader.* Kansas City: Beacon Hill Press.

Bradberry, T., and Greaves, J. (2009). *Emotional Intelligence 2.0.* San Diego, CA: TalentSmart.

Carnegie, D. (1936). *How to Win Friends and Influence People.* New York: Simon & Schuster.

Clance, P. R., and Imes, S. A. (1978). The imposter phenomenon in high achieving women: Dynamics and therapeutic intervention. *Psychotherapy: Theory, Research & Practice*, 15(3): 241–247.

Forni, P. (2002). *Choosing Civility: 25 Rules of Considerate Conduct.* New York: St. Martin's Press.

Goleman, D. (2005). *Emotional Intelligence: Why It Can Matter More than IQ.* New York: Random House.

Goleman, D., Boyatzis, R., McKee, A. (2001). *Primal Leadership: Unleash the Power of Emotional Intelligence.* Brighton, MA: Harvard Business Review Press.

Johnson, B. (1996). *The Joy Journal.* Nashville: Thomas Nelson, Inc.

Rohr, R. (2019). Economy old and new. Center for Action and Contemplation, November 30, https://cac.org/economy-old-and-new-weekly-summary-2019-11-30/.

Spain, S. (2017). Five takeaways from Condoleeza Rice at the KPMG Women's Leadership Summit. ESPN, June 28, https://www.espn.com/espnw/voices/espnw-columnists/story/_/id/19762601/five-takeaways-condoleezza-rice-keynote-address-kpmg-women-leadership-summit.

Chapter NINE
Principles of Negotiations

Think about this scenario, which plays out every day as a physician. We see a patient, make a diagnosis, and determine what needs to be done for the patient—meds, surgery, physical therapy, whatever. Then we are told that a specific medication needs prior authorization, or just prescribe an alternative. But there truly is no therapeutic equivalent. We won't compromise and will jump through the hoops to get the appropriate medication for that patient. Compromise? Accept less than my best judgment, just to save the insurance company a buck? No way! No compromise!!

Or maybe the approved insurance template or physician expert doesn't have my level of expertise to truly understand this particular patient situation. Or maybe that physician is out of date on the most current literature.

The whole idea of negotiations is a tough topic for physicians. Why would I have to negotiate when I'm right? And compromise?? No way!! This is one of the leadership areas where what we do as physicians is in direct contrast to what we must do as leaders.

Now go on down the road to enter the leadership arena. You have analyzed the situation, listened to the options, evaluated the alternatives, and have made your decision. And you are right. OK, you ARE right, but you are not a dictator or emperor. You don't get to throw down the gauntlet and state, "My way or the highway." That is the quickest way out the door with an election of a new leader. You MUST compromise. Ugh! You better learn the principles of negotiation.

The two topics of conflict management and negotiations are closely related but not identical. *Conflict management* frequently results in having to employ principles of negotiations. An important distinction must be made between conflict that occurs around a task and conflict that occurs in relationships. The first type of conflict, otherwise known as part of the task analysis process, is healthy and even necessary to good decision-making. See Chapter 5 (decision-making) for details on how to work through options. The second type of conflict that occurs in the process of intending to build relationships is deeply divisive and must be dealt with if the relationship is to go forward and be productive. Remember, the physician leader must negotiate and has to build relationships, both of which are requirements to be an effective leader.

When there is dissent in the organization, assume each faction is giving the right answer to a different question. What question is each trying to answer? Conflict is something good trying to happen—take that energy and put it to work. There is another interesting facet of conflict. Consider what you must learn in the conflict situation. Sometimes getting knocked around (figuratively) is the path to learning and growth. I have seen this play out in a situation where a person was the protege of a powerful leader serving as his de facto sponsor. There was nothing wrong with that relationship, but whenever the protege got into a conflict, the powerful leader stepped in and resolved the situation. This was very annoying to those of us who did not benefit from a similar relationship and sponsor. However, when the sponsor was no longer around, the protege was bowled over by later conflicts. He had been protected from learning how to deal with the issues. The sponsor was truly trying to help. But managing the conflict for the protege crippled the protege's ability to learn those skills. There are people who enjoy conflict. I'm not one of them. But learning how to deal with conflict is a growth opportunity.

There is a story about a butterfly that was in the pupa stage and just starting to push its way out of the pupa covering. A bystander was watching the epic struggle the butterfly was having to employ to get out of the pupa covering. Thinking he could assist, the bystander got a pair of cuticle scissors and cut the side of the pupal covering so the butterfly could get out. But the butterfly fell over, permanently crippled, as the wings were not yet ready to be released. What the bystander didn't know was that the very process of the struggle to get out of the pupa drove fluid into the wings, expanding them and making them functional. Without that struggle, the wings fell useless and the butterfly died. The struggle, hard as it was, was part of the growing process.

Amygdala Hijack

The first point to discuss in managing conflict and conducting negotiations is to understand the principle of *amygdala hijack*. It is very true that no one makes you angry – you GET angry, for a lot of different reasons.

I know we all took a neuroanatomy course, and you probably have a distant recollection of this part of the brain and what it does. It is the emotions center of the brain, also known as the reptilian center of the brain that develops as a part of the early embryological pathway of development. Daniel Goleman coined the term in 1996 in the first edition of his book about emotional intelligence (Goleman 2005), describing the emotional responses from people, which are immediate and overwhelming and usually out of perspective to the actual stimulus. That's because the stimulus has triggered memory of a much more significant emotional event/threat. It is also part of the "fight, flight, or freeze" pathway. The *hijack* part of the process occurs because this emotional center of the brain processes information milliseconds earlier than the neocortex/rational part of the brain, so the amygdala acts before any possible direction from the neocortex can be received to override the response. The further problem is that the amygdala hijack response can persist for a variable period of time—maybe 30 minutes, maybe more than a day. Every person I know (including me) has demonstrated the power of the amygdala hijack with the blistering email sent in haste and regretted at leisure. Thus, the admonition is to sleep on such emails before sending—be aware of the amygdala hijack in conversation and back away before irretrievable words are spoken. Get attuned to your body's reaction to a sensitive topic and learn to back off. Remember that you can't turn it off—you just must wait for it to dissipate. Or you will regret it. Believe me.

Thomas Jefferson said, "If you enter a discussion and become angry, then count to 10. If you are still angry, count to 100."

The "STOP" model is a good one to avoid reactivity.

1. Stop whatever you're doing.
2. Take three deep breaths.
3. Observe how your body feels.
4. Proceed with kindness and compassion.

Also look at the controlling drama the other person is using to try to control your response:

- Being nice and manipulative
- Being nasty and manipulative★
- Being aloof and withdrawn
- Playing the victim or "poor me" role

★These insults tell you about the other person, so go back to the issues, or if that doesn't work, just leave. Further, you can look at insults for clues to what they really think. Those insults are revealing much more than the perpetrator may realize.

According to Schwartz (2012), here are the five top amygdala triggers in the workplace:

1. Condescension and lack of respect
2. Being treated unfairly
3. Being unappreciated
4. Feeling that you've not been listened to or heard
5. Being held to unreasonable deadlines

These triggers also occur in the leadership arena, both in the leader and in those being led.

Negotiation Steps

One of the most famous writers on principles of negotiations is William Ury (Fisher and Ury 1983; Ury 1991). I will expand on his points below and refer you to his writings for more in-depth analysis. In this section we will look at his steps and follow that in the next chapter with specific techniques of negotiating. Please note, although Ury's books are about principles of negotiation, the approaches to managing conflict are highly applicable.

1. Separate People from Problem

We will sort through this approach in more detail below. So here is the basis of the issue. The relationship of the people (Chapter 8), whether good or bad, tends to get entangled with the problem. This is the unproductive type of conflict that must be dealt with, whether the relationship is good or bad. It may seem counterintuitive to say that good relationships can cause problems in negotiations, but consider that if you really like a person, you may be more willing to compromise on points in order to maintain that good relationship. And that compromise may not be the best possible for the situation.

The undeniable truth is that a bad relationship tends to lead to attribution of negative motives, and vice versa. So, you must disentangle the people from the problem. The best approach is always to be hard on the problem, soft on the people. Following are pointers on how to deal with the "people" part by employing the following approaches.

2. Focus on Interests, Not Positions

What does that mean? Interests and positions sound the same and are often used interchangeably but they are different. The best way I can explain it is that everyone has interests. A position is what one person has decided will fulfill that interest. The classic example is the two sisters who each want an orange, which is to be used right now. There is only one orange in the house. There is no option to obtain another orange in the required time frame, for purposes of this scenario. We will pick up this story a little later.

Remember, the more you present and discuss your position, the more you become invested in winning it. The more you try to convince the other side of the value of your opinion and your position, the more you become committed to it and don't feel you can or want to change. And that axiom applies equally to the other person in the negotiation. Go back to truly listening (see Chapter 2, Communication). Arguing over positions is inefficient, as just explained. And don't forget the lessons learned in Chapter 1.

John Kenneth Galbraith (1971) reminds us that "faced with the choice between changing one's mind and proving there's no need to do so, almost everyone gets busy on the proof." That sums up much of the reason why negotiation is so difficult.

Don't forget that the difference between the reality each person sees and what the reality really is, is the problem. Again, back to perception of the situation (see Chapter 4, Perspectives). Try to move to discuss different perceptions and verify the validity of those perceptions.

Even if it is a wrong perception, something is making that person see things that way. And who knows, you may be the person with the wrong perspective. When arguing with an idiot, be sure there are not two.

Another aspect when considering interests vs. positions is expressed in this quote from Colin Powell, "Avoid having your ego so close to your position that when your position falls, your ego goes with it" (Powell 2012, p. 12). That may be the crux of the matter regarding positions. It is really our ego that takes the position and defends it so strongly.

Here is another tactic. Pose this question: "If you were me, what would you do?" It is a good question to ask the other negotiator. It is not an enjoyable question to be asked. But do think about a possible answer.

I even saw this point done effectively by asking the questioner to change seats when in a power differential situation, in the powerful person's (your) office. Then have that person ask the question as if it was their job to prepare the response. This is not feasible in a group meeting but can be very powerful in a one-on-one meeting on your own turf.

3. Clarify the Interests

In the sisters/orange scenario above, one sister wants the juice to drink, and the other one wants the peel for baking. Each sister had turned her interest (juice or peel) into her position (my position is that the whole orange is needed for my interest), which is not the case. As anyone who grew up with a sister knows, the first approach to be employed is, "I want the orange!" So, look for ways to understand their perception/perspective.

Remember, conflict exists when the facts are viewed differently with different perspectives that have different implications. Remember the "6 and 9" drawing in Chapter 3.

Be very careful that you don't assume what they are going to do, especially based on what you fear they may do. Remember: you have fears too, and they must be considered.

Be very sure you don't attribute the worst motives to them (see Chapters 2 and 3 on Communication and Chapter 4 on Perspective).

4. Several Positions May Satisfy the Interests

In real-life situations, several positions may satisfy the interests if those interests are made very clear. For the sisters and the orange, the solution is simple and straightforward if they are willing to see the other's need. If the people involved are willing to clearly express their position and listen to another, there is room for discussion.

5. How Do We Identify the Interests?

It is important to ask, "Why do you want XXX?" or, "Why are you proposing this approach?" "What do you hope to achieve?" You need to get to the underlying interests if the other person will allow you to do that. Some of the most powerful interests include:

security
money
belonging
recognition
control

This is not an exhaustive list, and sometimes the person may not even be aware of what her/his interests are. Thus, the need to ask more questions. On the other hand, the person may be very aware of what her/his interest is and really doesn't want you to know. The best approach is still asking questions. "Asking questions" is covered in Chapters 2 and 3. Remember, this is not the time for statements/accusations/assumptions disguised as questions!

6. Invent Multiple Options with Mutual Gains Before Picking One Option

This step accomplishes several purposes. First, it leads to resolution of the negotiation. But perhaps even more importantly, it sends the signal that the other person's interest is valued; thus, the other person is valued. That simple approach speaks volumes about the intent of the leader and goes miles toward separating the person from the problem. At this point, the principles outlined in Chapter 5 on "Decision-Making" come into play. The options must be analyzed for positives, negatives, and unintended consequences. Don't assume there is a fixed pie to divide up. Coming up with reasonable options often means expanding the parameters of the discussion. That bigger picture may provide the basis for an additional option or two. Don't succumb to premature judgment (you might want input from a "P"—perceiving—in the discussion, from the MBTI personality type profile). This step simply can't be rushed.

7. Insist That the Result Be Based on an Objective Standard

OK, that is again easier said than done. Sometimes the standard doesn't possess a lot of objectivity. But seeking objectivity is better than leaving some nebulous platitude on the table, such as, "Let's see how it goes and decide what to do from there." What are we looking to achieve? By when? Give it a shot.

8. What Is the Next Step?

Just do it! If all these steps have been put in place, the actual final decision is already set up for success and acceptance.

BATNA

We have not talked about BATNA in this chapter. That is the "Best Alternative to a Negotiated Agreement." The whole point of negotiations is you must compromise. But it is not as simple as that. Here is the real question you must answer: "What will you personally accept?" You must know that ahead of time. When you are selling something for $20 and the potential buyer offers $10, it doesn't work to "split the difference" and agree on $15 when your actual cost of production is $17. Granted, it is often intuitive to agree to the concept of splitting the difference. But that assumes that the two starting points of the offers are equally acceptable, one just being more desirable to each person in the negotiation. The shrewd negotiator knows to position her/himself closer to what s/he wants than what the other person wants.

The only way to combat this strategy is to establish your BATNA. Further, the better your BATNA, the better your power. The position that "I get this, or I quit!" is more reasonable when you were planning to hand in your resignation anyway and you can use that point as leverage, since the other negotiator doesn't know about your pending resignation. And you have a contract for another position already signed, sealed, and delivered. "I get this, or I quit!" is a very risky BATNA for the person with no other employment offer on the table and a significant stack of bills due very soon. In the cost-based example above, your price is $20. Therefore, your BATNA must be $18 in order to cover your costs ($17) and allow a little wiggle room for negotiation.

When engaged in negotiations, be sure you are thoughtful about what information you share. I will never forget the time I was involved in a very-high-stakes negotiation situation. I clearly stated my objectives. The other person was also clear and wasn't budging on a couple of items. I wanted the deal to be successful and had worked out my BATNA. I was comfortable that we were in range, even though I wanted an agreement closer to my goal, naturally. Then something interesting happened. We were interrupted in the conversation by a staff person. We had to wait for a few minutes until the issue could be cleared. In that brief hiatus in the discussions, we had an uncomfortable pause in the conversation, the pregnant pause we discussed earlier. Then the other person started talking. The other person revealed why the points were of such importance to her. Turns out, there were some other people involved in the overall situation, of which I was not aware and who were not of importance to me. But they were very important to her. She had other reasons for completing the negotiation no matter what, so as not to disappoint others who were tangential to our discussion. Aha! Now when we came back to the subject negotiation, I suddenly had the upper hand, because even though she was still negotiating very hard for her points, I now knew that getting the deal done was more important to her than even getting those exact points agreed to, as she wanted them. She has just lost her negotiating advantage and she didn't even realize it!

Final caution: Be sure to look for the following tactics: misrepresentation, incomplete disclosure, applying stress, good cop/bad cop, threats, delay, ultimatums, and victimization. Do not use these as points for argument, to refute or to prove them wrong. Again, tactic perceived is tactic lost. When you recognize these tactics, they won't be effective. They can either be ignored or responded to later.

Takeaways for the Wise Physician Leader

While physicians don't compromise or negotiate because it likely affects a patient's health and safety, leaders don't often have such black and white situations to manage. The need for compromise must be considered; it is better described as negotiating. The first thing to remember in the often-tense negotiating situation is to watch for the amygdala hijack, yours and theirs. If you allow yourself to get hijacked, you have lost your negotiating position. The most commonly used steps of negotiation all center on deeper analysis and understanding. Bottom line: A negotiated agreement must meet the legitimate interests of each side, to the extent possible, resolve conflicting interests fairly, be durable, and take community interests into account. A lofty goal.

Scenarios and Questions

1. You are negotiating a new contract. You know the other negotiator from other interactions, which were never pleasant. What approach do you employ to keep yourself focused at the issue at hand and stay balanced?
2. You feel your heart starting to race and your blood pressure rising as the negotiation goes further and further away from your goal. What is happening, and how do you control it?

3. You are leading a negotiation, and all parties are clearly focused on positions, not interests. This has resulted in no one getting what they wanted or needed. How could that negotiation have been handled more effectively for all parties concerned?

4. A young leader has asked you to mentor her. You have set up your first meeting. She is very excited to tell you about a recent negotiation she managed. She is very proud of the outcome. In helping her to analyze her process, you ask about her BATNA. She doesn't know what that is. And the actual outcome didn't meet her financial goals. How do you guide her through negotiation principles to get a more appropriate outcome next time?

Resources

Fisher, R., and Ury, W. (1983). *Getting to Yes: Negotiating Agreement Without Giving In.* (B. Patton, Ed.). New York: Penguin.

Galbraith, J. K. (1971). *Contemporary Guide to Consensus, Peace and Laughter.* Victoria, BC, Canada: AbeBooks.

Goleman, D. (2005). *Emotional Intelligence: Why It Can Matter More than IQ.* New York: Random House.

Schwartz, T. (2012). Five Common Emotional Triggers. In *The Way We're Working Isn't Working: The Four Forgotten Needs That Energize Great Performance.* New York: Simon and Schuster.

Shell, R. (1999). *Bargaining for Advantage: Negotiation Strategies for Reasonable People.* London, England: Penguin.

Ury, W., (1991). *Getting Past No: Negotiating in Difficult Situations.* New York: Bantam Books.

Voss, C., and Raz, T. (2016). *Never Split the Difference: Negotiating as If Your Life Depended on It.* New York: HarperBusiness.

Chapter TEN

Conflict Management

I kept having repeated disagreements with him. He would make a statement and I would disagree with it. He further defended his statement and I further disagreed with it. It was a never-ending tug of war regardless of the topic, regardless of whose topic it was. If he said it, I opposed it. One day, I was a bit distracted, and when he stated his stupid, poorly thought-out opinion on an issue (you see the perspective I was bringing to the discussion), I didn't respond. The look of surprise on his face was priceless. I kept quiet. After another couple of such statements to which I did not respond defensively, he stopped making his points. Amazing! A few days later, he started a similar discussion. Having considered carefully the earlier sequence of events, I did comment this time but very noncommittally, "Oh, I see." Not confrontational, not oppositional, not supportive, just noncommittal, acknowledging I had heard him. In a few more days, he finally stopped trying to get me to take the bait. Astonishing! It is like a wrestling technique where you push and push back against the opponent and then suddenly pull away, and the opponent falls over. There was nothing left there to push against. Try it. Carl Jung famously said, "What you resist, persists." And the opposite as well. This is an interesting dynamic. When you push for a specific point it frequently prompts the other person to push back. *When you stop pushing, so do they.* This is one of my favorite techniques for managing conflict, technique number 20 to be exact.

Twenty Techniques for Managing Conflict

Let's look at the full list of *techniques* of managing conflict. Some of these points will sound familiar. With the specific intention of repeating myself, the most important foundation for effectively managing conflict is to avoid the amygdala hijack, as described in the last chapter and expanded on in this one.

Utilize Clear Communication

Technique #1 is absolutely crucial in managing conflict: *Utilize clear communication.* Listening carefully can help you understand their concerns, identify their misunderstandings, and clarify their fears. Remember, the last thing is the real thing. Don't shut off the discussion until they have fully presented their concerns. And don't forget the pregnant pause. Let them fill the void of silence. If you need to speak, do so only to clarify your understanding of what they are saying. See the Chapter 2 discussion of the importance of definitions.

Remember the OMS3 class president story? I was furious with him for what I had been told he had done. My amygdala was definitely hijacked, and I let him have it. And blew it. I lost my moral authority and my leadership as the adult in the room. I had to apologize for my outburst. It would have been totally unnecessary to have gotten into that situation if I had utilized Technique #1 above.

Fredrik Backman in his book *Beartown* says, "One of the first things you learn as a leader, whether you choose the position, or have it forced upon you, is that leadership is as much about what you don't say as what you do say" (Backman 2017). I would have been wise to follow that approach with my OMS3 class president.

Maintain a Positive Outlook

Technique #2 is easier said than done: *Maintain a positive outlook.* The easiest way to do this is to implement what is called "going to the balcony." Think about it. If a fight breaks out between the two people standing next to you and you chime in, you are very much part of the problem and may get drawn into a significant degree. But if the fight breaks out when you are up on the balcony looking down on those two, you are much less likely to get drawn into the fray. And you can keep a more positive attitude. OK, we don't have physical balconies in a negotiations situation, but we can all have mental ones. Zingers may even be shot your way, but if you are on the balcony, they seldom reach you and therefore won't hit you. At the very least, you will have time to duck, so to speak, so you don't let that comment hit you at your core. Don't let a personal attack spear you. It is being shot your way to exact a specific response, not usually aligned with your best interest. Let the "spear" go to the problem. Remember, raising your voice in an argument lowers the chance for reconciliation and indicates that you didn't go to the balcony because the spear hit its target. And by then, you know you could have done a better job managing the situation.

Here's another thought. How many steps to your balcony? This is my idea, which helped me visualize that the more invested I am in a position or option that is under attack, the more figurative steps I may need to take to "get to the balcony." It's another way of saying "deal with that amygdala hijack." When an idea near and dear to my heart is under attack, it is going to take me longer to quell the amygdala hijack (more steps to get to the balcony) than when it is a casual thought without my personal investment.

Admit Your Own Mistakes

Technique #3: *Admit your own mistakes.* Being vulnerable and personally opening up in that way often spurs others to do the same. Always take the high ground. It also lets the other negotiator understand you are bringing humility to the discussion, not seeking arrogant dominance, which is usually not a successful approach.

Let Them Save Face

Technique #4: *Let them save face; don't drive the other person into a corner.* Just feeling they have no options can force them to take a much firmer stance than otherwise is appropriate or necessary. You always want the other side to be happy or at the very least heard and appreciated. If they are unhappy it sets them up to try to make sure the negotiation fails. This approach is also a corollary to #3 above.

Look Forward, Not Backward

It is never helpful to bring up old slights and hurts, which seldom apply and just enflame emotions. That's why we have Technique #5: *Look forward, not backward.* That is very *anti-balcony.* Almost always hijacks your amygdala and theirs.

Express Emotion

Technique #6: *It is OK to express emotion and to let others to do so as well,* without blame, because it is legitimate. It is OK (and necessary) to allow venting, just don't react with the same yourself. This point is a little different than the amygdala hijack. It is also very well established that if the other person is not allowed to vent, the rest of the discussion can't proceed. And their venting – let's call it description of the problem from their perspective – must be listened to without response, argument, defensiveness, and without disputing their "facts."

Respect Yours and Others' Fears

Technique #7: *Accept the fact that fears are fears and must be considered.* Including yours. Diminishing the significance of another person's fears can be very disrespectful. If they didn't think their fears were real, they wouldn't be fears.

Attitude Can Alter Relationships

Technique #8: *Whenever you're in conflict with someone, there is one factor that can make a difference between damaging your relationship and deepening it. That factor is attitude.* "Your attitude and beliefs will have a huge impact on your ability to resolve the conflict" (Stark 2013). Well put.

Don't Acquiesce

Here is another interesting tactic that may have been used on you in the past. Technique #9: *If you offended the other person and you truly weren't being offensive, don't acquiesce.* This can represent another ploy to make you feel obligated to give in to the other person, since the purported "offense" deserves accommodation. Not if you truly didn't offend. Be careful, because this whole "perspective" thing points out that what may not seem offensive to you may be offensive to another person. That is also part of the problem with employing humor; it can be easily misunderstood or misdirected, or offensive. Bottom line, this is a very tricky point. Be careful as you go down that road.

Never Attribute to Malice What Can Be Explained by Incompetence

Technique #10: *Never attribute to malice what can be explained by incompetence.* This is a variation on the earlier point of giving people a good reputation to live up to, stated in a funnier way. There may be a more innocent explanation for the poor decision than an intentional plan to sabotage a proposal.

Differentiate between Helping and Being Used

Technique #11: Remember, *you must differentiate between helping and being used.* Once again, those two positions can be very similar. Trust your gut.

Reframe the Image

Technique #12: *Look for opportunities to act INCONSISTENTLY with their perceptions, also known as reframing.* Send a different message than expected and get them to think differently.

"What does that mean?"

Let's say the other person states "I know you don't like XXX." The best response is, "Actually I do like XXX very much, I'm just not sure it is the most appropriate choice to be used in this setting." That puts a different perspective on the discussion and takes the proverbial wind out of his/her sails by diminishing the impact of this perceived like/dislike. It is an effective response approach known as *reframing*.

Here's another approach. Consider reframing your natural anger into sadness in a negotiation situation. Let's say you are naturally angry about the brick wall of opposition you are hitting. Instead of expressing your appropriate anger, you could reframe as, "I'm so disappointed we aren't getting to our shared goal of XXX." Not accusatory, not pointing fingers, just sadness. Shared feelings of sadness can lead to cooperative concession-making; oppositional anger often leads to an impasse.

Another way to use this technique of reframing is when given an excuse, respond, "That is exactly the reason you *should* do XXX!" You are acting inconsistently again, and this time in response to a purported excuse. In both cases, the other person is making assumptions about you and your opinions, and you are turning the tables. It may seem difficult to turn what on the surface looks like a very plausible excuse into a position which is 180 degrees opposite. However, remember that nothing is black and white, so there is always an element of an excuse that matches your purpose. For example: A committee member repeatedly declined to attend a national meeting that all were expected to attend at least every other year. Her reason always boiled down to, "I'm too busy working on such important projects, I can't afford to take the time away to attend." Instead of arguing, the best response may be a variation of "that's exactly why you ought to go! You need to share your strong work with others and help the community see some new perspectives." She went.

Another use for reframing is to determine ahead of time what the big picture looks or ought to look like. Then consider what points you want to make. After the other person has made their points, and you have clarified your understanding, move to their side of the argument. Remember the drawing of the "6" and the "9"? Different people in different places saw different things. How much more powerful would the person seeing the "6" have been if s/he had stepped to the other side of the drawing and said, "I see the 6 AND the 9!" Big picture!

Set the Agenda

Technique #13: *Don't let the other person set the agenda as they would so like to do.* If the other person comes with a set of arguing points, most of which you disagree with, it is human nature to respond by going down their list and countering every point. It is hard not to. But consider that you have just let the other person set the agenda, craft the perspective for the discussion, and limit the topics and perspectives to be discussed. If they ask a question and you answer it and they ask the next question and you answer it, they are running the show and they are in charge.

This caution is a variation of the admonition for you to "go to the balcony." What is your perspective? What do you wish to achieve? What do you wish to accomplish? In other words, what is the big picture here? The big picture will inevitably address the other person's points but not in their order or with their emphasis. You will frequently see politicians do this; some are better at it than others. They will be asked a question and they will answer with their list of talking points, most of which are not directly related to the specific question. The truly artful negotiators will respond with, "I'm really glad you asked that question because it helps us focus on the big picture, which is ..." And the original question is never directly answered. Or at least not in the order or with the emphasis the questioner intended or would like. Plan what message you want to get across and go there.

I watched a master of this technique field a question about a new policy that wasn't going over well. Rather than be defensive, she took the discussion to a higher level of why they were there in the first place, the excellent educational experiences they were having, how much the faculty cared about them and their education, and on and on. She didn't ignore their concern. She didn't diminish their concern. She just brought a big picture perspective, which was truthful and fully applicable. I watched in amazement as she literally turned the attitude in the room around 180 degrees. Masterful.

Assume They Agree

Technique #14: *Assume they agree.* Even better, ask them several questions that start with points to which you both agree and move to points to which you wish to have them agree with you. The idea is to get them saying "yes, yes, yes" so that when you get to the hard questions, they are already used to, and committed to, saying yes.

Make Their Decision Easy

Technique #15: *Make their decision easy and along the lines you have chosen.* An example would be to ask, "Do they want the blue shoes or the brown shoes?" not whether they want to buy ANY shoes.

Ask Questions and Pause

Silence will force the other person to keep talking. Technique #16: *Ask questions and PAUSE!* It is very hard to keep silent, but it is very effective. (See "pregnant pause" in Communication Chapters 2 and 3.)

Recognize When They Have Already Said Yes

Technique #17: *If they are still talking, they have already said yes; they just don't know it yet.*

"Really!?! But aren't they going to keep talking and continue to try to convince you of their opinion?"

You can still work with the person who is still talking to you. There is no other option when the person has walked away or hung up the phone on you. You can do the same and walk away, but you have lost your access to the person who can get to the answer you want.

Employ Precision Thinking

Technique #18: *Employ precision thinking.* Watch for this tactic as well and don't fall for it. You will hear a gross generalization stated with great confidence. Which likely has no basis except in that person's perception, especially that desired by that proponent. When encountering the following statements, reply with the statement in parentheses, which pursues the desired precision.

"Things are bad" ("compared to what?")

"They say" ("who says?")

"I can't" ("yes, I understand that, and what if you could?")

"Always" ("really?")

Seldom are any of these statements absolute, and the speaker knows that or is quickly reminded of it. When you ask for precision answers, you quickly establish the weakness of their argument. When your intent is to convince the speaker of a different perspective, the precision-seeking questions still need to be spoken kindly with acknowledgment of the validity of such a concern, still pushing for the precise point.

Ad Hominem vs. Ab Hominem

Technique #19: *Ad hominem vs. ab hominem.* Don't fall into this trap, either. The most common usage of this Latin phrase is the first half, *ad hominem*, which means "to the man."

"OK, but what does that mean?"

It means, "I don't like this person, so I don't like her/his ideas, regardless of how well thought out and appropriate to the problem." This is a dangerous trap to fall into, as it colors how we interact and respond. It is also very hard to avoid. It is a variation on the bad relationships setting, discussed above. There are always people who have found our negative "buttons" and have learned how to effectively "push" them. Then later, they have a response, recommendation, or request and you can't see the request for the "trees" of dislike generated by the earlier interaction.

This also works the other way, but I have never heard it cited in the same manner. I may also be inventing this phrase, as I don't find it in any source. But it still makes sense and makes my point. *Ab hominem* would mean that I will attribute more weight and significance to the opinion of someone I like as opposed to someone I don't care for. It is human nature. The point is that an argument made by someone I like will be given more weight than an argument made by someone I don't like – simply because I like the person – with less consideration of the actual merits of the two positions.

Stop Pushing

Technique #20: *Stop pushing and your opponent will eventually do the same.* See the introduction to this chapter.

All the above are techniques or tactics. Ury (1991) reminds us, "*Tactic perceived is tactic lost.*" Watch for the points listed above and be sure they aren't being used on you. For example, people may get angry in order to get you to do what they want. That is very hard for someone who doesn't like confrontation to deal with, but it is a ploy to be recognized and prepared for. If you detect they are trying to make you angry in order to get you to agree, it becomes much easier to not take the bait. It becomes much easier to stay on the balcony. They are trying to get you to be angry and lose your thoughtful approach; therefore, you will become more likely to lash out and say something you will regret later. I was in a meeting where we were trying to deflect and resolve conflict. My sparring partner starting using some of these techniques and tactics, which I recognized. I smiled to myself. Tactic detected is tactic lost. Thank goodness!

Difficult People and Difficult Conversations

This is an important point for leaders. Every leader runs into "difficult" people. People who won't listen, people who bring up points that seem unrelated to the issue at hand, people who won't give any consideration to a great idea. It's hard to remember, difficult people are in difficult situations. It is also likely that the leader won't know what that situation truly is. But remembering this point puts issues and people in perspective! Remember, you may be your difficult person's difficult person. Ouch again!!

Here are another couple of pointers about conflict management.

Give up needing to be the smartest person in the room. Suspend your need to defend a point of view. Walk away if necessary. See the experience as an evolutionary opportunity. Resonate compassion.

Another way to think about conflict management is as a difficult conversation. Difficult conversations are never about getting the facts right; they are about perceptions, interpretations, and values. The best explanation of how to understand and approach difficult conversations is the book titled *Difficult Conversations* (Stone et al. 2000).

1. *Usually, there is a disagreement about what happened or what was expected to have happened.* And as I said above, more often the conversation is about perceptions, interpretations, and values. Intentions of the participants are also important, although usually assumed and generally wrong. Difficult conversations don't involve feelings, they are *about* feelings. Refer to Chapter 4 on perspectives as those points are never more applicable than in difficult conversations. Remember, understanding the other story doesn't mean we have to agree. Initially unexpressed feelings can and usually will burst into the conversation and can make it difficult to listen. "My sense is that you and I see this situation differently. I'd like to share how I'm seeing it and learn more about how you're seeing it." Other examples of neutral responses: "That's a different perspective." "I see your point of view." "That's something to think about."
2. *Listen well.*

"How many times do you have to remind me of that?!"

I don't know! Are you listening well?

A good resolution will usually require each party to accommodate somewhat to the other's differences, or perhaps to reciprocate, going one way on some issues and the other way on others – in other words, mutual caretaking or negotiations. See Chapter 9 on Negotiations.

Sometimes there are just differences that won't be resolved and still be honored. The know-it-all person believes that knowledge is the answer to any problem and will keep pushing "the data" without hearing that the discussion is not about the data. Don't let that person be you.

3. *In some leadership situations, it may be necessary to acknowledge their feelings.* This is not always necessary in leadership, unless the situation has become tense. It is critical in medicine as all doctors know that the last thing mentioned by the patient is the real thing and tears tell the tale. In leadership, acknowledging is not agreeing, and it helps both speakers understand the significance of what is being said. Nonverbal communication goes beyond what people say; it reveals what they feel.

4. *Demonstrate respect for the other speaker.* Respect means truly valuing the other speaker. Respect helps the other person understand that s/he is seen as legitimate. That the other person has legitimate boundaries. That the other person has real potential. Even though the speaker may be younger, less educated, or earlier in the education continuum, that person is bringing her/his perspective. It still may be wrong or less applicable in the bigger picture, but being wrong and being disrespected are two different things.

Another aspect of the respect point is the question, how can they walk out of this and look powerful? This is also known as *saving face.* It is important not to push the other person into a corner with no way out. Letting her/him save face is critical. If you push so hard the other person's only option is to skulk away, the discussion isn't over, you just don't know it yet. And the future won't be pretty. On the more serious side, Machiavelli said if you have the option of offending someone or killing them, you must kill them as you will be forgiven. But the offensive action will not be forgotten or forgiven. Luckily, we are not in the sixteenth century, but his point about offenses turning into grudges is still true.

5. *Remember, it is very important to hold off on making judgments about the person and the conversation.* In other words, put on hold the temptation to fix, correct or problem-solve what we see, so we can begin to inquire into what we observe, and accept that we have a grip only on uncertainty, not on certainty. Access your own ignorance by recognizing and embracing things you do not already know. Develop the ability to see what is happening as it is happening. And adjust as appropriate and

as necessary. This is particularly challenging for physicians because our medical approach is to problem-solve and fix things and people.

6. *Finally, be very careful what you say in a difficult leadership situation.* This is your opportunity to reveal what is true for you. Remember, that may not be what is true for the other speaker. There is a very effective way to do this that is very persuasive. We'll cover the approaches to effective persuasion in Chapter 11.

Rules: Yours or Mine?

Determining the rules of the game is another point in conflict management! It took me awhile to figure this out, and I haven't really seen this perspective written up in this way. One of my sisters explained it to me. We all have our own rules – for life and for life's experiences. My sister drove up to the bank's drive-in window and was behind a couple of other cars in line. The first car in line completed the transactions and left. The second car in line didn't move up right away and she saw the driver's head down, engaged in what appeared to be preparation of paperwork for the next bank teller. The driver soon saw that the lane was open and moved up to the window, still appearing to be preparing the required paperwork. My sister became more and more frustrated at the lack of preparation by that driver. Then she stopped to think. Her rule was that you don't go up to the bank window until you have the paperwork ready. That didn't appear to be the rule of the driver ahead of her. And it wasn't written down anywhere that this was the bank's rule, either. Frustrating as it was, it was still just HER rule (and maybe a lot of other people's unwritten rule as well). We all have our own rules. The point is you must know yourself well enough to know that you have rules. Then you must recognize that if you have rules, it is likely that those whom you are choosing to lead also have rules. And just because the rule is only in my mind doesn't make it any less important or any more negotiable; maybe simply, less flexible.

The thing about rules is, they keep popping up in conflict situations. You are probably breaking the other person's rules about how they see that things are supposed to be done. The problem is, you don't know what these rules are! But you can easily break them, nonetheless! With consequences!

Takeaways for the Wise Physician Leader

Don't let your amygdala get hijacked!!
Points such as…

> Listening is critical.
> Stay ethical above all.
> Focus on the big picture.

…lead the list of 20 techniques to employ in conflict management.

Don't forget that difficult people are in difficult situations. And the principles from the book *Difficult Conversations* should be memorized by all physician leaders. Lastly, you have unwritten rules that other people break. Just be aware that you are breaking their unwritten rules as well.

Scenarios and Questions

1. You are in a conflictual situation. You listen and then admit the mistakes you have made that contributed to the conflicts. What kind of response did that candid and vulnerable approach generate?
2. You are trying to persuade the other person to engage with a specific plan which they obviously don't want to. They react with lots of excuses. What is an effective way to respond?
3. Your neighbor down the hall in the office gets really upset when you have a box outside your office door, even for a few minutes when you are getting ready to go to a meeting and you don't have time to put it away. He sends angry emails and has complained to HR. He is restricted to an electric scooter and your office is between his office and the bathroom. Why is he being so difficult?
4. What are the unwritten rules of behavior you bring to the conversation? How often do people break your rules? Do you ever break what appear to be others' unwritten rules? How can you approach this situation by responding with precision thinking questions?
5. Your team keeps bringing up their fears about a topic. They are truly groundless fears. Why won't they listen to your assurance and just go on? How do you help them do so?
6. The team member stormed into your outer office and blasted your staff. Your admin came into your office to let you know that the person

is coming back to your office and is still upset. When the team member comes into your office, she is calm and considers the options you present. What happened?

7. You are in a discussion and the other person won't consider your suggested options. You finally get frustrated, as you have done all you can and offered all the feasible options, and finally say, "This is my final offer; take it or leave it!" How did that work?

Resources

The Arbinger Institute. (2015). *The Anatomy of Peace: Resolving the Heart of Conflict* (2nd ed.) Oakland, CA: Berrett-Koehler.

Bolton, R. (1986). *People Skills: How to Assert Yourself, Listen to Others, and Resolve Conflicts.* New York: Touchstone.

Cartwright, T. (2003). *Managing Conflict with Peers.* Greensboro, NC: Center for Creative Leadership.

Fisher, R., and Ury, W. (1981). *Getting to Yes: Negotiating Agreement Without Giving In.* New York: Penguin.

Patterson, K., Grenny, J., McMillan, R., Switzler, A., and Maxfield, D. (2013). *Crucial Accountability: Tools For Resolving Violated Expectations, Broken Commitments, and Bad Behavior* (2nd ed.). New York: McGraw-Hill Education.

Patterson, K., Grenny, J., McMillan, R., and Switzler, A. (2011). *Crucial Conversations: Tools for Talking When Stakes Are High* (2nd ed.). New York: McGraw-Hill.

Schwartz, T., (2012). Five Common Emotional Triggers, in *The Way We're Working Isn't Working: The Four Forgotten Needs That Energize Great Performance.* New York: Simon and Schuster.

Stark, P. B. (2013). Attitude is king in conflict resolution. peterstark.com, posted April 29, 2013, https://peterstark.com/attitude-conflict-resolution/.

Stone, D., Patton, B., and Heen, S. (2000). *Difficult Conversations: How to Discuss What Matters Most.* New York: Penguin Books.

Ury, W. (1991). *Getting Past No: Negotiating in Difficult Situations.* New York: Bantam Books.

Chapter ELEVEN

Persuasion

"It is important to be more persuasive, not more correct."
—Abraham Lincoln

"One of the best ways to persuade others is with your ears
– by listening to them!"
—Dean Rusk

"It is difficult to get a man to understand something when his
salary depends upon his not understanding it."
—Upton Sinclair

These are all good quotes on persuasion, our next chapter in our roadmap.

I will tell you a story of which I'm not very proud but makes my point. We were waiting for the bus to transport us to the hotel where we would be staying and where the training would occur. Well OK – not a lot of training would be going on, but there would be a mandatory educational session about the drug Tenex from its manufacturer, A. H. Robins. My husband and I were on the bus full of physicians and spouses who had been flown from Phoenix to San Francisco and given a sales pitch on the use of Tenex. We were all then treated to a nice long weekend of seeing the sights, enjoying the cuisine, and seeing a live show. All on the drug company's tab. OK, make that on the patients' tab, as the cost of this trip was factored into the price the patient and insurance companies would pay.

That was the only drug company junket we ever went on, and it was over 30 years ago. I wish I could claim that it was due to my reassessment of the appropriateness of such trips and a clear-eyed view of the inappropriateness thereof. Truly, it just didn't feel right. I declined any future invitations from other companies (it was a common practice in the day). Subsequently, those types of trips were prohibited. A prescribing doctor cannot receive any such expensive inducement to prescribe a drug.

Now you can say, was I asked to prescribe that drug? No. Was I asked to select that drug in preference to other, less costly alternatives? No. But suffice it to say, I had a fondness for that drug in my practice. To the exclusion of alternatives? No. But was it easily thought of when the options for a patient were considered? Yes. I told myself that I was not being influenced by that drug company and that trip.

The thing is, the power of this type of persuasion technique is so strong that not only are such trips now prohibited but so are coffee mugs and even pens and pads of paper listing the name of any specific drug. I still have a stash of old drug company promotional pens and do-dads, just to show students what such relics looked like. The truth is that what I tell myself with all scrupulous integrity and what is going on in my brain in this arena, which is unbeknownst to my conscious thoughts, are two different things. A 2017 study published in *JAMA* suggests that even such small gifts can cause doctors to change their script-writing habits. This is called the *reciprocal pull* or an example of the principle of reciprocity. It is one of the principles of persuasion.

These nine principles of persuasion come from the work of Robert Cialdini, PhD, Arizona State University (Cialdini 1984). *Influence: The Psychology of Persuasion* became an instant best-seller and is still required reading for most business schools. He gathered his data by going undercover and taking sales and marketing jobs at a used car lot, a fund-raising organization, and a telemarketing company. He catalogued and analyzed the types of tactics he saw and tested their veracity. Rather than just list the principles, I am going to tell you about an experience where several of these principles were used on me.

Not only are there principles of persuasion, there are also techniques of persuasion. First, we will look at the principles.

Principles of Persuasion

The following experience demonstrates well the principles of persuasion. I was at the American Osteopathic Association national convention and visited the exhibit hall. I try not to engage any salesperson in the exhibit hall; I just want to see what is there. An extremely persistent salesman trailed me nearly halfway across the sales floor, offering me a tiny packet of body lotion, and thus began the full-on press to persuade.

Reciprocity, Friends, and Expectancy

Despite declining several times, he finally said, "It's just a little packet of body lotion." OK, I accepted one, actually two, just to make him go away. Well that didn't work. Getting me to accept it was his plan and I fell right into it! Little did I know, he now knew he had a promising prospect. He said, "So let me show you how this lotion works." I was sunk! He was invoking the principle of reciprocity. See my Tenex experience above. As the JAMA article pointed out, even small gifts encourage a positive response of reciprocity. I accepted a very small gift and now I felt obligated to hear at least a *small* portion (I hoped) of his spiel.

The first thing he did was spread the lotion on my hand and have me feel how nice it went on and how it was not greasy. Then he said, "Try some!" And then he promptly proceeded to spread it on half my face! **Principle #1, Reciprocity**, was in full swing.

Just then a couple of my friends walked by, and as soon as they said hello and I responded accordingly, he called to them, "I hope you enjoy your new body lotion." They smiled and said they really liked the lotion. He was tying into persuasion **principle #2, Friends,** and **#3, Expectancy**. You are more likely to do what your friends do, or more formally, what they ask you to do. In this case, they were affirming the value of this product. Expectancy says you will try to get the results your friends get.

He understood the impact of peer pressure. Friends are very persuasive.

By now, the salesman had pulled out an instrument that he said would take that wonderful lotion and facilitate it absorbing into the skin to remove my wrinkles. Wrinkles?? Ouch. It was a handheld warming and vibrating instrument that he rubbed all over the part of my face that already had his lotion on it.

After about five minutes, he asked if I saw an improvement in the wrinkles on the treated versus the untreated side of my face. The answer was maybe yes, but it was also very clear to me that he had produced a little localized and short-term swelling in the skin due to heat and pressure, which would make any wrinkle (as if I had any) appear less prominent. He could see that effect on my face wasn't having the desired effect on my pocketbook, so he said, "I know you probably aren't interested in this instrument. It costs $4700." Not now, not ever. That seemed like a pointless exercise on his part, and then he said, "Of course the lotion only costs $300."

Contrast and Association

Principle #4, Contrast. Now I get it! When you are putting two significantly different things together, it makes them look even more different. He was trying to promote the idea that he understood that $4700 was WAY too much, but by contrast, $300 was a mere pittance. This is also known as *anchoring*, providing a reference point as a basis upon which to compare. Just initially telling me the lotion cost $300 would have closed the conversation right then and there. He hoped that the contrast in price was sufficient to promote the relatively inexpensive purchase of the lotion. Believe me, it did not. But it was a good try, using the principle of contrast.

Then he said, "You know, I was just in Las Vegas, and Beyoncé really likes this lotion!" **Principle #5, Association**. Endorsements do work. Tom Selleck pushing reverse mortgages, LeBron James pushing McDonald's, Shaquille O'Neill pushing whatever he is pushing today. There is a reason that celebrities are hired to promote products.

Scarcity

By now, I was interested in seeing what principle he would try next. I didn't have to wait long. He stopped a minute and looked around at his booth and said, "You know, I don't have very much lotion stock left. I hope I have enough for you!" **Principle #6, Scarcity** – limited quantities are more desirable. How many times have you heard, "Hurry, this offer is good only while supplies last!"?

Consistency and Conformity

Principle #7 Consistency: We try to stick to what we said, even if wrong. How to use this principle? Ask someone questions to which they would be expected to say yes. Keep asking similar questions. Finally, you get to the tough question they would previously have to stop to consider responding with yes or no, and yet, once they get in the rhythm of saying yes and will likely inadvertently blurt out yes, that consistency principle works in your favor, as you knew it would. Once they have said yes, they are much less likely to turn around and say, "Oh, I meant no," as that demonstrates indecision and lack of clarity about the issue, neither being admirable characteristics to reveal in negotiations. I have heard people later admit, "You are right that wasn't a great idea, but I already said yes, and I hate to change my mind, as it makes me look indecisive." My smart salesman used a variation of this technique. He kept asking me questions that had yes answers, sort of. Did the lotion feel nice on my hand? Yes. Did I see a difference in the side of my face with the lotion as compared to the side without? Yes, sort of.

Those are all the principles he employed. But there are a couple more, from Cialdini's work.

Principle #8, Conformity: People like to go with the majority. Years ago, there were ads for cigarettes stating that 9 out of 10 doctors smoked Camels! This ad was a combination of the Association Principle (from those influential doctors) and the Conformity Principle. Very few people in the day thought smoking was a bad idea for your health, so if such a high percentage of such an influential group of people chose this cigarette brand, that was persuasive enough for the observer to do the same and conform with the majority.

Power

Principle #9, Power, specifically power perceived, is power possessed. It has some similarity to the association principle. The US president has power. Your state's governor has power. The hospital CEO has power. The hospital chief of staff has power. That's not the only type of power. There is also power that is perceived and can be equally influential, if not more than the official power. The physician thought-leader on the medical staff or medical group has power. The retired and beloved, wise physician leader still has power. Those last two individuals provide examples of power that is not possessed for any official reason, but carries significant perceived power, thus the "possessed" power. Bottom line, power of any type can be used to persuade.

Those are the *principles of persuasion.*

Techniques of Persuasion

Here are *techniques of persuasion.* Just to be clear, these techniques are used to make the principles of persuasion successful.

Enthusiasm and Passion

I have paraphrased Aristotle over the years about the likelihood of success in making an argument by emphasizing either the words, the logic, or the passion. Words and logic are important, but the most persuasive of the three is passion.

Many enthusiastic people have carried the day, simply because of their enthusiasm and passion. I've found that while it's almost impossible to succeed without enthusiasm (regardless of how smart or gifted you might be), it's also quite difficult with enough enthusiasm to fail. It's that important. Keep that in mind as you listen to other speakers and the passion they bring to their presentations.

Compassion

Demonstrating *compassion* for those touched by the topic can also be very persuasive by showing the very human engaging and attractive side of the presenter.

Attitude

Remember, the attitude you bring to a discussion is more important than whether or not you like the person you are talking with.

"Wait a minute. I thought you said you loved every role you ever had?"

Yes, every role, but not every person I encountered in each role. But I still followed this approach. The situation deserved a good attitude, including that directed to the individual, even if I was not very fond of that person. Sometimes my opinion changed, sometimes it did not. But I didn't have to climb out of a deep hole created by my hijacked amygdala if I never went there in the first place.

Persistence

How many times has a parent given in to a persistent child's request, just to shut them up? 'Nuff said. Here are some tips on persistence:

- *Agree with your adversary as soon as possible* by acknowledging her point of view. That approach validates her and stops her from having to persuade you of her value. Then you can move on to the bigger and more important issues.
- *Acknowledge the value of the other person.* I don't see this done very much, but when done it can be very effective. I was recently on an interview panel and one of the candidates was graciously responding to each panel member as they introduced themselves. When she came to me, I introduced myself and the interviewee said, "Oh, I know who you are. I've heard about you from one of your biggest fans!" Turned out, I knew a family member. I can't say it changed the outcome of the interview, but it was very disarming. Also, it was a little embarrassing, but the words and affirmation couldn't be taken back. Professor John Dewey said, "The deepest urge in human nature is the desire to be important" (Carnegie 1936).
- *Be wiser than other people if you can, but don't tell them so,* Lord Chesterfield told his son (Carnegie 1936). Very wise advice. I must admit this one is sometimes hard for doctors. We are smarter and hopefully wiser on

a particular topic, based on our education and experience. And it feels like it can tip the scale in favor of our position if we remind others by subtly mentioning our credentials. What we sometimes miss is that this can come across as pretentious or arrogant, moving the scale in the opposite direction. Watch it as you proceed down that road.

Consider How You Are Presenting Your Perspective

You can make your audience sympathetic first, with your choice of frames. These are also known as anchors, primes, and mindsets. Frames are the mental models we use to make sense of life. They also shape the potential solutions. Even a small change in wording will change the choices. Every physician understands the difference when explaining the risks of a procedure. Doing this procedure will save 30 percent of the people. Or when doing this procedure, there is a 70 percent mortality. It is therefore wise to consider competing frames and decide which one to use to avoid restricting the options.

Ask them to help you and they become responsible for you. This seems counterintuitive, but it is a very strong technique. It is as simple as it sounds. It seems like asking someone to help you makes you beholden to them, and it does, but it also makes them more engaged with you. I have seen it used this way. You have a manuscript, and you would like an expert in the field to review it. That person has a reputation of not doing that very often. So, you tell the expert that you have a manuscript and you know s/he is very busy, too busy to review it. But as the expert in the field, s/he may know others who work in this field and who may have time to review it? Then you are not asking that person to commit any time to your project. But few people will decline to recommend an alternative reviewer after such a compliment.

What comes next is very important. Ask for the desired reviewer to make an introduction to the alternative reviewer. Or at least provide that person's contact information to you. At the very least, you can honestly say that the desired reviewer recommended the alternative reviewer. This is also very flattering to the alternative reviewer, with very little political capital expended by the desired reviewer. And sometimes the desired reviewer offers to look at the manuscript, even though not requested to do so.

Again, what happens next is very important. Provide your contact information and ask, "If other names of good reviewers come to mind, could you please let me know?" The desired reviewer has now become responsible for you, when, if asked directly to perform the review, the reviewer would likely have said no and that would have been the end of it. This is a really powerful strategy. Try it.

Give the other person credit for being smarter and more aware than they actually are. Another way to state this is, "Give the other person a good reputation to live up to." Say, for example, "I know you really care about ..." when you may not be convinced that is the case at all.

Give credit when NOT due and you are giving them a good reputation to live up to. This is a classic principle from Dale Carnegie. Another way to express and employ this principle is, "When you counsel someone, you should appear to be reminding him of something he had forgotten, not of the light he was unable to see," Baltasar Gracian wrote in the 1600s (Gracian 1992).

Some phrases that are also very persuasive:

"I wouldn't tell you what to do..." then you can proceed to tell them exactly what to do!

"Now, don't think I'm asking you to..." which is exactly what you are asking them to do.

"You might want to consider..." which is exactly what you very much want them to consider.

Takeaways for the Wise Physician Leader

There are several well-researched principles of persuasion you can employ: reciprocity, wishing to do what your friends do, employing an item of significant contrast to emphasize the differences, promoting consistency/conformity, and using power to persuade. Several techniques of persuasion can be used with those principles. The point to remember is that you should be aware of these principles and techniques both as tools you can use and as tactics others might use to persuade *you*!

Scenarios and Questions

1. Your colleague at work gives you some ballgame tickets he can't use. A week later, he asks you to buy some chocolates his son is selling as a fund raiser. What persuasion principle is being employed?
2. The restaurant menu lists an item priced over $100. All items on the menu are quite pricey but not close to $100. What is this principle of persuasion?
3. The popular movie star advertises a medical product with no connection to any expertise she might have. Which principle of persuasion is being demonstrated?
4. You ask for a favor or advice from a person with a much higher power differential compared to where you assess your power. How did that person respond? Did you get the favor/advice requested, or were you rebuffed?
5. You have said that you would go to a conference and now you review the agenda and see that the speaker you particularly wanted to hear has canceled. But you already told the team you were going and persuaded them to attend. Which principle are you employing if you still attend?

Resources

Berger, J. (2020). *The Catalyst: How to Change Anyone's Mind*. New York: Simon Schuster.

Carnegie, D. (1936). *How to Win Friends and Influence People*. New York: Simon and Schuster.

Cialdini, R. (2006). *The Psychology of Persuasion and Influence*. New York: William Morrow.

Cialdini, R. (2018). *Pre-Suasion: Revolutionary Ways to Influence and Persuade*. New York: Simon and Schuster.

Gracian, B. (1992). *The Art of Worldly Wisdom*. (trans. Maurer, C.). New York: Currency Doubleday.

Hogan, K. (1996). *The Psychology of Persuasion: How to Persuade Others to Your Way of Thinking*. Gretna, LA: Pelican Publishing.

Lo, B., and Grady, D. (2017) "Payments to Physicians: Does the Amount of Money Make a Difference? *JAMA*. 317(17):1719-1720.

Chapter TWELVE
Managing Change

Machiavelli is not the most admirable character in history, but what he wrote about how change works holds as true today as it did in the sixteenth century.

My paraphrase of his writing goes like this: "When you propose a change, you have weak supporters in those who might do well under the new system and strong opponents in those who did well under the old system."

That is SO true!

Change is hard and destabilizing, so people are often willing to "stay with the devil you know, rather than the angel you don't." Of course, that assumes that all changes are "angels," and seldom is that dichotomy so sharp.

Here are more quotes about change:

- "Why are we more successful? We are better at change." Sam Walton, founder of Walmart
- "Change is inevitable except from vending machines." Anonymous
- "Everyone thinks of changing the world, but no one thinks of changing himself" Leo Tolstoy, author

- "When it comes to change, we are always faced with the same choice: embrace or suffer." Anonymous
- "We will always have change; we won't always have improvements." Anonymous

As we begin this chapter, there are two different change situations we will consider. There is change that you choose to promote and implement (what you chose to change) and there is change that you find in the circulating milieu to which you must react (what someone else chose to change that affects you). First, let's explore how to approach making a change that you choose to promote and implement.

When You Are the One Who Wants to Implement the Change

Here is a story about the first step in implementing a desired change, creating/identifying a sense of urgency. I also told this story in Chapter 5 on decision-making, particularly addressing a crisis. When I became dean, I had studied the varieties of different curricular presentation models and was pretty sure I knew what would be the best one to implement. It should have been no surprise, however, that a new dean, not known to the faculty, and especially having never been a dean before, would not be accorded the privilege of implementing a new curriculum. Especially since this venerable COM had a high board pass rate, excellent application numbers, and a seasoned faculty. So, I tucked my virtual "tail between my legs," and deposited that curriculum-change plan onto the back burner. Now, fast-forward to the next set of board scores that came out in a few months. Guess what? The CCOM board pass rate, which had always been one of the highest in the nation, dropped to 2 percentage points below the mean. Unheard of!! Some faculty immediately asked to meet with me and asked what I wanted to put in place to turn this sad situation around! Now, this crisis grabbed everyone's attention and we were able to make immediate changes (not a full curriculum overhaul, mind you, as there wasn't enough time) that resulted in the scores popping back into their usual stellar territory. THEN I had the faculty's attention to look at an alternative curricular delivery method.

Don't let a crisis go to waste! In other words, establish or utilize an already created sense of urgency!

Eight Steps to Making Change Happen

John Kotter has written the most-often-cited book on this topic, *Leading Change*. His principles are universally cited as a well-established approach to making change happen. Here are his eight steps.

Step 1 Establish a Sense of Urgency

Kotter says, "Visible crises can be enormously helpful in catching people's attention and pushing up urgency levels. Conducting business as usual is very difficult if the building housing the business seems to be on fire."

If you are going to seek to change behavior, you must change belief (see Chapter 4, Perspectives). They must change to keep or get something of value. The sense of urgency pushes the situation into assuming a priority perspective. This principle is sometimes termed *the burning platform*. This point is the key to why my attempts at curricular change didn't work the first time around and then did carry the day the second time. I now see that I had no chance of persuading faculty to change the curriculum just on my request. I had not established a sense of urgency and could not do so, because there was none. I wish I had this roadmap back then!

Step 2 Form a Guiding Coalition

It is wise to *form a guiding coalition,* and as powerful and influential one as possible. Here is where early adopters come in handy. These people are willing to give something new a try. It is also important that they are influential in the situation, which immediately draws the attention of the others in the group. The leader's willingness to listen to other perspectives and incorporate aspects of those perspectives into consideration will go a long way to obtaining agreement with the change.

Step 3 Create a Vision

It is easier to get a response to a vision instead of a problem. This point speaks to the observation that people are not likely to follow a negative leader, at least not for very long. The person who just keeps pointing out the problem doesn't create the energy needed to create the solution. The problem will get their attention, but to have effective change, there must be a vision of what can be the alternative. There does have to be clarity on the goal and the general approach. Then it's time to develop the strategies needed to implement the planned change.

Step 4 Communicate the Vision

Participants in the group immediately start to think three things:

1. What do you want me to do?
2. What's in it for me?
3. What do I have to give up?

They may still be persuaded by the sense of urgency (Step 1 in the Kotter sequence). They may be engaged with the vision (Step 3). They still need to know the implications of that vision and what it means for them and their constituency. New behaviors may also be required, as modeled by the guiding and influential coalition (Step 2). The better the team understands the reasons for the change and the perspectives that are the basis for the current situation and the need for that to change, the more likely people are to accept the change. The communication process can be time-consuming, but it is critical to the success of the change.

Step 5 Empower Others to Act on the Vision by Getting Rid of Obstacles to the Desired Change

This is a very general statement that has varied applications in different situations. If there is a regulatory restriction involved in the change, that needs to be addressed. If there are insufficient funds in the budget, then a source of funding needs to be identified. If a previously and recently approved process is already in place and will need to be changed, that needs to be dealt with. If a previously approved process has already had funds expended which now cannot be recouped, the new proposal must address that situation, too. See "Sunk Costs" in Decision-Making, Chapter 5. Now is the time to smooth the road for risk-taking and for nontraditional ideas, activities, and actions, facilitated by the sense of urgency (Step 1).

Step 6 Plan and Create Short-Term Wins

It is very important to plan and create short-term wins, to move the vision forward. If the players can't see anything happening, especially early on, it is hard to keep them focused. This is an important point. When the US Congress approved the Affordable Care Act (ACA), for example, the Obama administration immediately put in place some attractive provisions that they could attribute to the ACA. Then the administration set the stage to anticipate even more attractive pieces of ACA to come. The best example is the provision that allowed young adults to remain on their parents' health plans until age 26. This piece of the ACA was very popular, encouraging support for future pieces of the legislation yet to come, some of which were not so popular. Someone in the ACA planning process had obviously studied Kotter's principles.

Step 7 Consolidate the Improvements Made

Work to consolidate the improvements that have occurred and be able to produce more change. This speaks for itself. Getting the short-term wins allows some breathing room to work on the more complicated parts of the change. There will now be increased credibility to change systems, structures, and policies that don't fit the vision.

Step 8 Institute More New Approaches

Finally, you will be able to institute even more new approaches, as change always moves in a spiral, seldom returning to where it started. While it doesn't always get to the exactly desired place, it will be a new place. You will likely also have identified new leaders in those who have demonstrated the ability to work in and promote the new system.

There are well described strategies to overcome resistance to change. It is important to diagnose the reasons for resistance which include parochial self-interest, misunderstanding, lack of trust, different perspectives on the situation and low tolerance for change. Approaches to deal with these causes of resistance to change are incorporated into Kotter's points.

Remember, change takes time and usually begins in the periphery. Also, remember that the people who need the most changing are usually the ones who resist it the most, often the late adopters.

A strong influence on making change happen is to consider the current culture of the organization. In Chapter 4, we discuss that change occurs more easily in an organization with a strong culture. Further, the impact of a toxic culture is described in the context of team members who won't raise important contrarian points for consideration. That's because it is well known that such comments will be perceived as unsupportive and thus are unwelcome.

"OK, if culture is this important to facilitate needed changes, how do you change the culture?"

You may not like this answer. The leader changes the culture by behaving according to the principles in this book. It takes time. Team members must repeatedly see that the physician leader acts with integrity, fairness, and is willing to make the hard decisions. I recall a comment from a faculty member, when I first became dean, that no student would be dismissed regardless of the severity of the infraction because that decision would represent lost tuition. No amount of assurance could convince him that would not be the case. Only by acting consistently and ethically, upholding academic principles over a couple of years, was I able to finally convince him that a culture of ethics would prevail, and the dean could be trusted. I led and our team implemented a change in culture.

Presentism

Here is another aspect of how you must view your current circumstances when you are planning to implement a change. The mistake is to think that how it feels now is how it will feel forever – how the current situation feels and how the current options feel is how it will be going forward. This applies to several situations, not the least of which is the amygdala hijack, but also in situations that require change. This is also part of a concept known as *presentism,* which speaks to the perspective that it is very hard to project what will happen in the future and what it will feel like. Yogi Berra said it well, "The only thing that is hard to predict is the future. Besides, the future ain't what it used to be." Who could have predicted smart phones 40 years ago, or the internet 50 years ago? Our tendency is to predict in a format known as "NOW, on steroids." In other words, how things look now, just more so. It goes back to the black swan concept. You can't predict what you can't imagine. It is also called "adaptation" – we get used to things as they are and take them for granted, thinking they will stay essentially the same. The lesson here is to understand that how things look and feel now are not what they will look and feel like in the future, even if we can't predict what that may be. No one would disagree that the emergence of COVID-19 is a classic case in point.

Change is not static.

"Ok, that seems really basic."

Yes, so when you accomplish one goal, you would think that you would then progress to the next goal on your priorities list, right? Nope. You need to reassess your priorities. Whether or not you are promoting change, you are living in a swirling world of change not created by you.

When You Are Dealing with Changes That Are Occurring Around You

Now let's look at the changes that occur around us or in the milieu in which we live and work. We all see that the world is changing very fast and not just because of COVID-19. We have always had generationally based changes that generally confuse the earlier generations, and are intended to do so. Overall, the pace of change for all generations is increasing exponentially. It can be useful to analyze change or reverse engineer Kotter's sequence.

The circumstances and your needs may have changed or progressed in the time since you set the first priority to be addressed and put that implementation process in place. And as I have said earlier, you can't step into the same river twice. And there is another factor here. When you created your priorities list before implementing and then completing priority item #1, you were able to see the circumstances where you were. Think of your progress through life as if you were walking through a wooded area blanketed in dense fog. You can see two steps in every direction. You make the best decision based on what you can see in that two-step radius – two forward, two backward, and two to each side. Now you have selected which direction to take and have completed priority #1 and have stepped forward two steps. Now you can still see two steps forward, backward and to the sides, but because of the fog, you now see different things than when you were in your previous position. There are new options that you may not have considered before. On the other hand, consider that those may be exactly the same options that were always there, but you had no way of knowing that because of the fog. I counsel people not to make rock-solid decisions about plans for the future because of that darned fog. I have constructed an acronym for FOG: Have <u>Faith</u> that the <u>Future</u> holds more <u>Options</u> and <u>Opportunities</u> to reach your <u>Goal</u> – you just can't see them yet.

When I was in grade school, I thought I would be a farmer's wife in rural Indiana. In high school and college, I thought I would be a medical technologist and work in a lab. When I went to medical school and residency, I thought I would be a general internist in practice for the rest of my career. When I became a dean, I had finally wised up to the fact that other opportunities would come along that I wasn't aware of at that time. And guess what? They did and they have. And circling back, every single one of those options and opportunities involved change—unpredictable, horrible, wonderful, exciting, challenging change. You can be a champion of change or a victim of change. There is just one thing you can't avoid: change.

One other caution. Just because it is important now, doesn't mean it will be important in the future. Don't forecast or anticipate that just one thing is going to change.

Takeaways for the Wise Physician Leader

Kotter's principles for leading change are the most well researched on how to manage and promote change. Progressing through his eight steps will make a significant improvement in the leader's ability to make needed changes. Further, the changing milieu in which we live and work is inevitable. It requires your attention. The circumstances around your leadership issues will keep evolving. However, behaving in an ethical manner will help create the culture you desire and facilitate the needed changes. Predicting the future is very challenging due to the principles of presentism and FOG. Because change is difficult to deal with doesn't mean it can be ignored. Or I should say, ignore at your peril as you proceed down that road.

Scenarios and Questions

1. You need to implement a change in your organization, and you are met with resistance. What is the first step you need to employ?
2. Which of Kotter's principles could have been of assistance in overcoming that resistance?
3. Why do we need to establish a sense of urgency? The change makes perfect sense; isn't that enough to have it accepted and make it happen?
4. Does the change that is occurring in a situation happen only because of a sense of urgency?
5. Is there an existing guiding coalition which you may be able to join in an organization's project to have influence?
6. Think of a recent change that was implemented in your organization. How was the change assessed, reshaped, refocused? These questions assume the change is intentional, which is not always the case. Still, going thru this analysis process brings the opportunity for insight.
7. We are making changes in the exact same milieu that was in existence yesterday, so we don't need to consider what might happen if the milieu itself changes too. Or do we?? What is this principle called?
8. You have all your options laid out. You have done the analysis and set out the plan—only to find out in a few months that there were a couple of other highly desirable options you hadn't heard about. What principle is in play here?

Resources

Bunker, K. (2008). *Responses to Change: Helping People Manage Transition.* Greensboro, NC: Center for Creative Leadership.

Kanter, R. (1983) *The Change Masters: Innovation and Entrepreneurship in the American Corporation*. New York: Simon and Schuster.

Knoster, T., Villa R., and Thousand, J. (2000). A framework for thinking about systems change. In R. Villa, J. Thousand (Eds.), *Restructuring for Care and Effective Education: Piecing the Puzzle Together* (pp. 93–128). Baltimore: Paul H. Brookes Publishing Co.

Kotter, J. (2012). *Leading Change*. Boston: Harvard Business Review Press.

Kotter, J., and Schlesinger, L. (2008). Choosing strategies for change. *Harvard Business Review*, July–August, pp. 130–139.

Machiavelli, N. (2008). *The Prince and Other Writings*. New York: Fall River Press (originally published 1532)

O'Toole, J. (1996) *Leading Change: The Argument for Values-Based Leadership*. New York: Ballantine.

Chapter THIRTEEN
Meeting Dynamics

Amazing things happen in meetings.

"Yeah right, boring things!"

OK, we tend to think of meetings as just providing the opportunity to sit down, decide what to do, and leave. Oh, it is so much more than that! Those things do and must happen, but in much more nuanced and impact-ful ways than would appear on the surface. It's called *group dynamics* or, more specifically, *meeting dynamics*.

We will look at what to do before the meeting, where to sit, when to speak, how to gesture, and what to do after the meeting, and consider the importance of how to dress in a meeting. This section of the roadmap has not been well researched, so there may be different detours you can also successfully pursue while traveling on this road. These road signs are based in large part on my experiences and observations.

How to Dress for Meetings

I wish I could say this point was not important, but it is. And it falls with more impact on women than on men. You must consider what you are wearing.

You only get one chance to make a first impression, and that first impression sets the stage for future interactions. A wise piece of advice I have heard repeated several times: Dress for the position you want, not the position you have. Don't think that "this time it doesn't matter." You never know who may show up at a meeting or be an associate of someone you wish to impress. Sloppy, dirty, worn, ill-fitting, or unstylish clothes that are not dressy enough all send the wrong message. You don't have to be a fashion plate. You just must show that you care enough about this meeting to bring your "A" game. Notice I didn't say "too dressy" was a bad idea. You can always dress down, but if you came to the first meeting dressed too casually, you have a hard time "dressing up." It's not fair; it just is.

Before the Meeting

Remember, the real meeting occurs before and after the meeting. It is absolutely critical to prepare before the meeting.

As the leader, you need to determine some key points. For example, what exactly are the goals to be achieved by holding this meeting? Does this meeting even need to be held? Who needs to attend? What is the time frame allotted for the meeting? Do you need to prepare a timed agenda? A timed agenda is especially useful if there are many items to discuss in a short time, and it signals to the attendees that you will be aiming to stay on schedule, unless diverted by a more pressing or complicated topic. It also makes it very clear who is in charge of the meeting.

If a decision is to be made, if possible, find out what the participants think before you get to the meeting. The need to do that varies directly with the impact of the decision being made. No need to say more on that point.

Even if you are not the leader, there is significant planning involved. Find out who is going to be there. Find out the agenda of the meeting. Then determine your role, what you wish to accomplish in the meeting and whether the other attendees are aligned or opposed to your perspective. It is critical to be punctual to pick your seat.

Where to Sit

Where you sit is critical. If you are the leader of the meeting, you need to sit at the head of the table, wherever that may be perceived to be. Sitting with your back to the door in a one-door room puts you at a disadvantage if someone comes late or leaves and returns. So, sit where you are at the perceived head of the table and pick the best view of the door/s.

If you are the leader, you need to consider using name plates/cards that you put in place before the meeting and note the considerations described below.

Here are some general principles. If you are or wish to be aligned with the leader, sit to their right hand. That is the best place to have influence on the leader as you can have small side conversations or comments just to the leader. After that, it is the seat to the leader's left. That sequence would be reversed if the leader is left-handed.

If you wish to confront the leader or another attendee, sit opposite her/him. Not only are you sitting opposite physically, you are being and are perceived as oppositional. The seat at the opposite end of the table from the leader's seat is the second most powerful position after the leader's. A thoughtful leader who is expecting such a tactic may also choose to remove the chair from that end of the table.

The corners of the table are the next power positions as those seats give you a view of all the other attendees. The least powerful positions are at the middle sides of the long table, as they are good places to hide.

If you wish to minimize the impact of another person in the room, sit as close to that person as possible. Side by side of course, but CLOSELY side by side. Here's an example where sitting very close worked out better than sitting in a "power" chair. And I was very new to this organization's board, anyway, so not likely to get a shot at a "power chair." I was running a little bit late when I got to the meeting room. The seating was very tight in order to squeeze in the required number of chairs. There was only one seat left in the room, and it happened to be right beside the person I was most likely to tangle with in this meeting. I can't tell you how much I dreaded heading over to sit there, but there was no choice. Imagine my surprise when my opponent didn't say a word during the meeting! I spoke my piece and still he never said anything in response. I have seen the impact of this simple rule over and over, and it never ceases to surprise me. It's a variation of the aphorism, "Keep your friends close and your enemies closer."

A further consideration: Sit between the person chairing the meeting and the person whose opinion you oppose and whom you wish to influence to your way of thinking. It keeps the opposer from influencing the chair as much as you do.

Further, don't sit back and away from the table. It makes you appear uninterested and arrogant.

What if the table is round? Again, sit as close to the chair as possible, to have influence, sit opposite who you want to fight with, and sit to the right of the person you want to influence and have alignment with.

When Should You Speak?

It is never wise to speak first, regardless of your role in the meeting.

If you are the leader, you are wise to not present your point of view until near the end of the meeting. This is a very critical point. It is important to wait to hear some other perspectives and you may learn something new. And you will have a chance to gauge where the energy in the room is going. You will find out the direction of the conversation and what the opposition might be, as well as where it is coming from. If the leader speaks first, other ideas may be squelched. If the leader wishes to influence the group toward a specific decision and speaks first, they may miss the fact that the group was already convinced of that perspective and much time was wasted covering "conquered" ground.

If you are not the leader, you should plan to speak about third or fourth, or at about a quarter of the way through the meeting to show you are engaged and participating. Plan to speak again every 10–15 minutes to demonstrate your further engagement. Make your comments short and clear; consider them as a sound bite. Much impact is lost with a rambling, unfocused, vague comment. It may also be appropriate to ask questions, if they are pertinent and make sense in the flow of the conversation. You also don't need to speak on every subject, so if there are several items on the agenda, choose wisely.

What Do You Need to Say?

Consider contributing something about which you are confident, and that is new and maybe even controversial, to the other participants. It is always effective to bring a different perspective or observation that demonstrates you have done your due diligence. Taking the discussion to the 30,000-feet level is also effective. Saying something like, "When we consider this issue in light of the bigger picture of what we are working to achieve...." demonstrates that you have a full grasp of the impact of the discussion. And it may also demonstrate that you have bigger perspectives that others have not considered, making you a more valuable contributor now and in the future. It can also pull a meeting out of a hole that is being dug by getting too much into detail and missing the overall goal. Determine the "one thing" you want to talk about. Focus on making no more than three talking points.

"What if I can't think of anything to say?"

If you truly can't think of anything new to say, you can always chime in with something like, "I think Susan has a good point that we really ought to consider. Have we reviewed the full implications of her point?" It is important to demonstrate that you are paying attention and are staying engaged. Don't fall into the trap of saying, "I agree," period. Do that a few times and people will start to discount your input as noncontributory, even when it truly is!

How to Speak

Here are several pointers for you to consider:

- Never ever actually say that you are nervous! It doesn't take you off the hook, it identifies you as an amateur and puts all your comments in doubt.
- Do say something like, "As physicians we all..." That establishes a sense of camaraderie and agreement and provides a basis for collaboration.
- Whenever possible, work a new person's name into the conversation in order to help you remember it. It also makes that person feel more part of the group.

- As a leader, you will find that when a group of people laughs, each member of the group can't help but make eye contact with the person they feel closest to. You will learn which members of the group are bonding and learning to trust one another.
- Speaking with excitement and passion makes other people like you and become enthusiastic themselves. This is not always appropriate, but when it fits the situation, it is a very effective way to help build consensus.
- Regardless of your role in the meeting, be positive, prepared, and professional. As we have discussed elsewhere, people only follow positive leaders in the long run.

Speak Slowly

"The basic rule of human nature is that powerful people speak slowly and subservient people quickly—because if they don't speak fast, nobody will listen to them."

Attributed to Michael Caine

Gestures and Stance

The communications principles from Chapter 2 apply with the additional caveats:

- *Don't cross your arms.* You will come across as arrogant and having made your mind up already.
- *Don't touch your face.* You will appear to be hesitant, uncertain, and indecisive.
- *Don't turn away from the speaker.* You will be seen as disengaged and uninterested.
- *Do maintain eye contact.* You will look more serious and committed to your point.
- *Do lean forward and focus intently on the other person when he or she is speaking.* You will demonstrate that you are engaged.

- *Consider making a "tent" of your fingers/hands*—it makes you look thoughtful and ready to make valuable input.
- *Smile specifically in response to what others say or do,* rather than grinning nonstop. Only the novice grins nonstop and nervously.
- *Open hands are seen as more engaged,* as opposed to a fist, and also create more trust.
- *Arms that are unfolded make you look more open to conversation.*
- *Nodding your head during a conversation or when asking a question makes the other person more likely to agree with what you're saying.* As with smiling, don't do it all the time or it loses its effect.

Remember, you can't fake gestures, at least, not for very long, without looking contrived.

Following are some more pointers when standing and talking with meeting attendees before or after the meeting.

Keep your elbow at your side when shaking hands, drawing the other person closer than arm's length. Being closer is more engaging, but there are times when you want to keep the other person "at arm's length," as it were.

When standing, be sure to *stand erect* with shoulders squared, balancing your weight evenly. Some people demonstrate their nervousness by squirming or getting into a contorted position, which is not advisable.

Another curious point. You may notice that people's feet point to you if they are interested and listening to what you're saying.

Addressing People in Meetings

The related practice in a group setting of calling women by their first names and men by their titles is unacceptable. A slip-up that is immediately corrected is one thing; a consistent discrepancy in the use of titles vs. first names is not to be tolerated. The challenge comes when such a practice is occurring in a setting of a distinct power differential. The woman being called by her first name may choose to reply to the speaker by addressing the man by his first name. If it is too intimidating to call the leader by his first name, she may elect to call another male member of the group by his first name, repeatedly. The offsetting balance of the informality is that people like to hear their own name and it increases the persuasiveness of the point being made.

Such a discrepant title/first name situation may require some offline conversation. Pull the leader aside during a break or after the meeting to say something like, "You may not have noticed, but it felt to me that you were calling all the women by their first name and all the men by their title." This is an example of "giving them a good reputation to live up to," which implies that the discrepancy was an oversight and not intentional. Again, if the power differential is significant, the women may need to engage another person, man or woman, who has more power in the organization, to serve as a sponsor and bring the discrepancy to the leader's attention. Again, it's not "fair" but can't be ignored, either. This type of situation is addressed further in Chapter 14.

Wrapping Up the Meeting

Be sure these next steps are clearly understood by all meeting participants and accompanied with an appropriate timeline. As the leader, conclude the meeting with the following items being clearly determined. This is a list like the one presented in Chapter 5, Decision-Making.

- What was decided?
- What steps have been agreed upon?
- Who is in charge of/tasked with what steps/processes?
- What is the timeline for accomplishing and reporting each specific goal? The next meeting date may not be the appropriate reporting time, either too late or too early.
- What are the resources available to accomplish the goals? Are more resources required?
- What obstacles need to be addressed in order to facilitate the plan?
- Who are the team members or other individuals available to work on each goal?

Remember, as leader of the meeting, don't let the meeting participants delegate up. Sometimes it is easy to volunteer yourself as the leader to handle some of the tasks. That is not a good idea, for several reasons. First, you need to learn to delegate. Second, you need to turn your attention to other items that only you as the leader can do. Third, other members of the group need to learn how to do these tasks. Even if they may not be as experienced in a specific task as you, the leader, might be, they still need to try it out and learn. Fourth, other members of the group may have further good ideas they can put to good use in their assigned tasks.

I first saw point #3 in play at a pageant at my church. We were preparing a small video trailer advertising the pageant to be shown at our various services and sent to other nearby churches. One of the church members had a well-known locally based video company, and he offered to prep our little video for free. The pastor graciously declined and selected one of the staff to oversee this project. He had very little experience in this area. As I was known to do, I called the pastor and asked about the wisdom of this decision, turning down the experienced successful company who had offered to provide this service for free. His answer? "The video company already knows how to do this. Our staffer needs to learn. What a perfect opportunity for him." Well there's that! And he put together a very credible trailer.

The Meeting Is Over

When the meeting is over, it isn't really over.

You need to solidify your points with those with whom you concur. Be sure they know you appreciate their support and have yours. A brief chat at the end of the meeting is wise, if feasible.

Even more importantly, when you defeat a person's closely held position, immediately go to that person following the meeting to connect person to person. You may have disagreed on a policy point, but you don't need to be disagreeable in general. And even if you weren't disagreeable, you still need to be sure that person is affirmed as a person. You don't want to inadvertently create an enemy. The point upon which you disagree this time may lead to a point where you agree next time. You don't want to generate resentment from this meeting such that the person will disagree with you in a future meeting, just to be contrary. And don't you do that, either!

I was recently in a brainstorming meeting where another participant in the meeting and I kept bringing up different points that appeared to counter each other. This was a particularly influential individual with whom I didn't agree, but since I had never met him before and could foresee opportunities where we could work together in the future, I was looking for ways to connect with him, even though we weren't bringing the same perspective to this specific discussion. Then I found it. He quoted a specific book several times. At the next break, I went over to discuss that book with him. At the following break, I bought and downloaded that book and gave it a glance or two. That gave me the opportunity to go back to him to discuss that book again. We were able to communicate on two different levels, that of the specific meeting we were in and that of shared appreciation for well-presented perspectives in said book. I couldn't diminish my points in the current discussion just to get his concurrence, but I also couldn't afford to lose the opportunity for engagement for likely future positive interactions for other purposes.

Finally, the meeting isn't over until you send a note or an email or make a phone call to close the loop. The final contact provides an opportunity to thank people for whatever contribution they have made. It also establishes the leader as a thoughtful and gracious person!

Takeaways for the Wise Physician Leader

There are many subtleties to a meeting. Not being aware of what is happening or ignoring what is happening doesn't stop those dynamics from occurring. Yogi Berra said, "You can see a lot by watching." The Wise Physician Leader understands that the way people behave in a meeting is far from an exact science but will likely give strong signals about what is going on in the meeting, far beyond the actual words spoken. Meetings must be considered thoughtfully—where you sit, when you talk, how often you talk, just to name a few things to review and plan. A critical part of the meeting occurs outside of the meeting, the follow-up. This includes not just who is doing what, but thanking people, clarifying comments, mending fences, affirming that the person who "lost" an argument is still a valued participant—just to name a few of the necessary after-meeting steps.

Scenarios and Questions

1. You are the leader; you got to the meeting late and must sit with your back to the door, as it is the only seat left. How do you compensate for sitting in this position and still remain in charge?

2. What if you truly are enthusiastic about an idea and really do want to speak first to get the group energized to agree with you? What are the upsides and downsides of that approach?

3. What if you really *are* bored at the meeting? Can't you sit back and daydream? Or check emails? You are a busy person! List some positives and negatives of that approach.

4. What if you are close friends with the leader who therefore persists in calling you by your first name? She calls all other meeting attendees by their titles. How should you handle this situation?

5. The meeting is over and one of the participants is obviously glaring at you. What do you do? Ignore the person? It's her problem! Or go over to engage her and find out what is going on? Which is harder? Which is more effective in the long run?

Resources

Knapp, M., and Hall, J. (2012). *Nonverbal Communication in Human Interaction* (8th ed.). Stamford, CT: Cengage Learning.

Chapter FOURTEEN

The Physician Leader as the Whole Person: Facing Discrimination

I walked into the ICU as a fourth-year medical student to start to pre-round on my patients. One of the cardiologists soon arrived. I can't say that he specifically directed his comments to me, but he loudly announced that it was too bad that schools took women as medical students who were just going to have babies, quit practice, and waste all that training. They were taking seats from perfectly good male applicants who would put their training to good use. Such comments were quite common on his part.

I applied for the internal medicine residency in this 550-bed hospital. Women had been residents in other specialties in that hospital, but not in internal medicine. I wasn't going to let that stop me. I applied, went through the rigorous interview process, and was accepted as the first woman to ever be a medicine resident at that hospital. Now it was time to set up each resident's rotation schedule. I decided that my first rotation should be with the cardiologist mentioned above. I would show him what a great job I could and would do. I worked very hard that month and knew he was aware of the quality of my work. I was treated fairly by him and his staff. The last day of the rotation, he took his wife/nurse and me to lunch, his usual practice. To my surprise, he handed me a large shopping bag. He encouraged me to open it and inside was a two-volume set of Brunwald's *Heart Disease: A Textbook of Cardiovascular Medicine* that cost a handsome sum of $175, especially back then. I don't know if that was a tradition for those who rotated on his service, but I was certainly stunned. He complimented my work and the residency progressed.

Now fast-forward to seven years later. I finished the internal medicine residency and had been in practice four years in another part of the United States. One day, my staff pulled me from a patient room because this same cardiologist was on the phone. He never says "hello," just states his name. Then he said, "I'm finishing my term on the American College of Osteopathic Internists (ACOI) board and I'm nominating you to take my place." I'm not even sure I had time to say "thank you" as the phone call ended abruptly, just as it had started. You need to understand that being a member of the ACOI board had almost always been reserved for the "old boys." And it took years to achieve the status to be nominated to this board. The previous year the first woman had been nominated and elected, so I would be the second woman on this board. Later, I was the first woman to be elected as president of the ACOI, and four more women have followed me as president, with several more having served on the board since my tenure. The cardiologist's nomination fast-tracked my progress—not only onto that board, but subsequently onto the national organized medicine stage.

Now fast-forward another 10 years. I was about to be inaugurated as the president of the American Osteopathic Association. I wanted to tell this story, so I called the cardiologist to ask his permission to do so. He readily agreed. Then I just had to ask, "So …. has your opinion of women in medicine changed?" He thought about it a minute and then said, "No, but you are the exception."

The role of women in medicine is a hot topic and is of high importance regardless of your gender, so I will present some of my perspectives and the current research. I must also assure you that there will be new research as soon as this book is published, so pay attention!

We all know the story of Elizabeth Blackwell being admitted to medical school as a joke and all the attendant circumstances she had to endure, when she showed up and performed at such a high level. The osteopathic tradition has followed a slightly different pathway. When Dr. Andrew Taylor Still started his osteopathic medical school in Kirksville, Missouri, he "opened wide the doors to women as students." He had seen the example of his mother managing the farm and a large family while his father was riding the preaching circuit, so he had learned that women were fully capable of functioning at a high level. That first class matriculated in 1892. Coincidentally, Johns Hopkins medical school was scheduled to enroll its first class in 1893. It was raising the princely sum of $7 million to build the school and hospital. When the fund-raising came up about $500,000 short, some of the leading women in Baltimore society agreed to fill in the gap, with one caveat—that women would be admitted as students on par with the male applicants. Let's just say, Johns Hopkins felt the heat and saw the light. Unfortunately, over the years the percentage of women students in DO-granting institutions gradually declined to match the percentage of those in MD-granting institutions. In the late 1960s, the percentages of women students gradually started to rise in both types of institutions.

Numbers of women and men students in all medical schools are now at parity. We temporarily achieved parity for the entering class in 2002–03, but the number of male students matriculating into subsequent classes dominated again until 2016–17. Looking at the percentage of women in leadership roles, we see that this percentage has certainly been lower than the percentage of women in the medical profession over the years. Many of us thought that disparity would resolve itself as the number of women in the pipeline approached that of the number of men. And we thought that the harassment and discrimination against women would also diminish with the equilibration of the numbers. Wrong, wrong, wrong.

So, there are three questions:

1-What is happening?
2-Why is it happening?
3-What can we do about it?

What Is Happening?

This is a critical question, as some deny that there is any discrimination against women physicians and women physician leaders, including being considered for progression into leadership roles.

The National Academies of Science, Engineering and Medicine Consensus Study Report titled "Sexual Harassment of Women: Climate,

Culture and Consequences in Academic Sciences, Engineering and Medicine" (Johnson et al. 2018) unequivocally documents that these issues have changed little over time as they are tolerated and overlooked, and that this harassment is worst in the field of medicine. Bottom line of their report is this issue undermines women's educational and professional attainment and promotes attrition from leadership roles, institutions, and the field in general. This issue has a stronger relationship with women's workplace well-being than any other job stressors. According to their studies, organizational antecedents have occurred due to having male-dominated and -led organizations with steep and vertical hierarchies as well as harassment-tolerant climates.

The issue of disparity has been presented in some attention-grabbing papers as follows.

The *British Medical Journal* published an article by Wehner (2015) titled "Plenty of moustaches but not enough women: cross sectional study of medical leaders," which found that women accounted for 13 percent of all department leaders at the top 50 NIH funded medical schools in the United States. Mustachioed leaders (yes, all men) accounted for 19 percent. That makes a major statement about representation.

The *Journal of Women's Health* published an article comparing how speakers at internal medicine grand rounds were addressed in their introductions based on whether the speaker and the introducer were female or male in the four different combinations (Files 2017). Female introducers used professional titles for over 90 percent of all speakers regardless of gender. Male introducers used titles for male speakers 72.4 percent of the time and first names for female speakers 49.2 percent of the time. The difference and the implications are striking. This point was discussed in Chapter 13.

Another finding from reviews of scientific meetings is the presence of *manels,* or panels that consist only of men. This is such a prevalent occurrence that many male physicians are now refusing to serve on a manel, or on a panel with only one token woman.

This gender bias extends to the names of medical society awards and to the gender of those who receive those awards. And there is another insidious aspect in the arena of awards. Why do we need an award specifically for the Woman Leader of "X" organization? You mean the women are so unqualified that they aren't competitive for the overall leadership award from the organization? Now, if there were a Woman Leader award and a Man Leader award, that would be different. I haven't seen any organization do that. However, I do understand that when the percentage of women in a particular organization is very small, highlighting women through such an award brings their contributions and even their presence to the forefront. That percentage disparity is not present in all such organizations with gender-specific awards, however.

So, this issue is real. Which prompts the next question. . .

Why Is It Happening?

Because this book is directed to developing physician leaders, I'm going to focus on the differences in how men and women are seen to function and ultimately lead.

The difference is well documented. Please note these are gross generalizations. Men are generally seen to function in a style called *agentic* and women are generally seen to function in a style called *communal*. Characteristics of the agentic approach include assertiveness and competitiveness with power based on position and authority. Characteristics of the communal approach include compassion, kindness, collaboration, and leading by consensus. Aggregated meta-analytic studies support the prevalence of these different gender-related approaches and conclude that men are better at managing tasks and women are better at managing people. The interesting contrast that has been seen is that if men exhibit aspects of the communal (collaborative) approach, they may get extra "credit," as this behavior is unexpected. As opposed to the situation when women exhibit that same approach, that behavior is expected, so not particularly noted or appreciated. Conversely, the man who speaks up (the agentic approach) can be seen as assertive and the woman doing the same can be seen as a control freak. Some have noted we have to "out-male the males." And women often still pay a price for doing that.

I personally have seen another aspect of this difference in approach. Two men seeking to come to an agreement while still maintaining their relative hierarchical status have been seen to sacrifice the agreement in preference to sacrificing their status. On the other hand, a man and a woman seeking to come to an agreement in a similar setting may choose, even without being aware of that choice, to bring both the agentic and communal approaches to the table, which allows/facilitates an agreement.

So, the fact that there are differences in approach has been documented, but why is there a difference in approach that appears to be gender related? The ancient conundrum of "nature vs. nurture" has been studied regarding this issue. The nurture side of the argument is bolstered by research that young girls are taught to play safe, smile pretty, and get As. The young boys are taught to play rough and swing high. Conclusion: "We are raising girls to be perfect, boys to be brave." Further studies show that young boys interact by conflict, honoring/respecting a strong hierarchy, fully understanding the guy on top gets all the privileges. The young girls interact through relationships, taking turns, making sure power is kept "dead even," with decisions being discussed and negotiated.

While there are few anatomical/physiological studies, a study has demonstrated that there are differences in the brain as measured by the functional MRI. Women who have been studied activate amygdalae more easily in response to negative stimuli, which would more likely lead to the formation of strong emotional memories of negative events. This reaction may lead women to ruminate over what has gone wrong in the past. On the other hand, women have also been demonstrated to have a larger anterior cingulate cortex, which recognizes errors, thus weighing options and scanning the horizon for threats. These differences are documented. What is not known is the relative significance and impact of the anatomical differences vs. the differences that have been nurtured. Correlation or causation? Further studies may have or need to be done.

There is another huge issue at play here. The reason I included the phrase "whole physician" in this title of this chapter is to recognize the disparate life roles that women and men physicians fulfill, bearing and raising children. It is true that women physicians have the wherewithal to obtain childcare and home support. It is also true that some women physicians wish to have the flexibility to choose how much and when to employ such support. My husband and I never had children, and the issue of infertility in women physicians has been well discussed elsewhere. That also means that I have no experience in making those tough decisions requiring balance of life and work. I recently congratulated a prominent woman leader as she is rising into a national leadership position. She is very accomplished and highly regarded by all the members of her organization. She related to me that during her most recent board meeting, she was again complimented on her knowledge and skills in leadership. Those compliments prompted her to ask her male president predecessors if they had to prepare for their presidential role AND to get three children ready for the changes that would occur in their life that year. You know that answer.

I don't have answers to guide women physicians and the male physicians who work with them, I just know that women shouldn't have to choose, shouldn't have to postpone leadership, shouldn't have to postpone childbearing. More male spouses of women physicians are choosing the home support role, which makes a huge difference. That's also not the right answer for every professional couple, but we must support women physicians as they craft the best answer for themselves and their families.

While it helps to understand what and why a circumstance exists, the most important question is, what can we do about it? That assumes that we as a medical profession in all genders want to do something about getting the best from all physicians in all roles we perform. That is our working assumption. I refer you back to the section on diversity, discussed in earlier chapters. Studies are very clear that the more diverse the parties engaged in any project, discussion, or decision-making function, the better the performance. So now the next question.

What Can We Do About It?

These are general approaches to promote fairness and equal treatment of women and all minority physicians, which will ultimately lead to more engagement and participation in leadership roles.

Everyone must commit to raising awareness of these issues. We must work together as different organizations and disciplines, all taking ownership of our roles and responsibilities. Further, we need to support those organizations that wish to improve their culture now. We must ensure that our own organizations don't populate our conferences with manels (panels with only men) or panels with only token women. The area of awards, who they are named for, and who they are awarded to, also needs thoughtful scrutiny.

On a personal level, we should each make a commitment to promoting fairness and equity. Each of us needs to assess our own personal bias profile.

Further, we need to be aware that we all make assumptions and may actually be making assignments based on those assumptions. It goes without saying that we need to influence our own organizations to have diverse and inclusive teams. The issue of how we inadvertently address people in meetings, some by titles and others by first names, has been addressed in Chapter 2.

I have brought my own prejudice to these questions. When I first became involved in organized medicine, there was a women's group named the National Osteopathic Women Physician Association. I joined, of course. Then I realized that this group had no power or authority or even any role in the larger membership organization, the American Osteopathic Association (AOA). So, I switched my activities to the AOA and eventually rose to a position on that board and was the first woman to be president of the AOA. I have modified my position somewhat, however. In talking to women who are in medical specialties with a fairly small representation from women, they are finding valuable support from organizations of women in that medical specialty to create a critical mass of women to gain the attention they deserve, as well as to develop the leadership expertise they need. I have seen this same dynamic work for the American Medical Women's Association, which provides a greater opportunity for women to learn leadership and advocacy skills, as well as advocate for women's issues.

When I graduated from medical school in 1981, only 15 percent of all physicians licensed to practice medicine in the United States were women. In my class, 12 percent were women. There were so few of us that we weren't even a blip on anyone's radar screen. In my case, all my classmates were very supportive, and I was elected vice president of my class every year in medical school. Yes, there were comments. See my opening story. Over time, I just did my work and was eventually elected chief resident by the residents from all the three internal medicine resident classes—again, first woman in that role.

I entered practice in a very different era, when almost all physicians were in private practice in the historically traditional sense. As I completed my residency, I was contacted by a physician who graduated the year ahead of me in our residency. The physician with whom he had been sharing call was leaving town and my residency mate invited me to come to MGH (Mesa General Hospital) to share office space and share call. I have related the story in Chapter 8 about how his sponsorship facilitated my development of a highly successful practice in very short order.

The perspective that is very different from the most common current type of practice setting now is I had a private corporation consisting of just me as a practicing physician. Every aspect of my practice was under my control, with the extremely critical and able assistance of my business-degreed husband. Not to mention my master's degree in Management with a specialty in Health care Administration. Other than splitting the cost of the office staff and overhead and taking calls 50 percent of the time, I determined how many patients to see in the office, which code to bill, how to process claims, how to follow up on insurance payments, what procedures to perform, how to conduct collections—every single aspect of my practice. I never worked as a physician for anyone but myself, never negotiated an employment contract, never had to compare my income with anyone else's, as I was the only person in the corporation. Medicare certainly didn't care whether I was a woman or a man physician. We were paid the same. So, when women now cite unfair employment practices, unequal salaries, and other evidence of discrimination, those are very real circumstances, but that was not my experience.

I have recently been asked to reflect on what kind and degree of financial discrimination I experienced when in practice, which didn't happen, and it took some thought to figure out why as I described above. We won't return to that world. In the day, my fellow women physicians and I weren't sweeping unfair employment issues under the rug; there were very few men or women physicians working in a setting where that would/could happen.

On the other hand, we thought that increasing numbers of women physician leaders would follow naturally as the number of women physicians in practice and in organized medicine reflected the increasing percentage of women in medical school and residencies. Not so. Still, I was the first woman to be elected chair of the hospital department of Internal Medicine, and chief of staff, for two terms, which didn't usually occur. Again, my motto was to do the best job I was capable of, and if that was not recognized, it was someone else's problem. I always had plenty of other things I could do and ways I could contribute.

This entire chapter deals with my experience as a Caucasian woman physician. I can only speak about the discrimination I experienced and therefore am best able to understand. However, I can extrapolate my experiences to those of physicians from all the other categories of minorities, and my basic admonitions fully apply. We need a diverse population of physicians to serve our diverse population of patients. This is on us!

Takeaways for the Wise Physician Leader

The title of this chapter includes the phrase "the whole person." This speaks to the point that men and women physicians are both "whole persons" with different approaches, skills, and responsibilities. I am not the expert on how to honor that wholeness, and certainly not how to advise others to do so. It is easy to say that all physicians can and must bring their "A game" to the task at hand. It will look different for each of us. We must ensure that happens, to accomplish our ultimate goal as physicians, serving our patients.

Scenarios and Questions

1. How can you ensure a more diverse representation in decision-making, which studies have shown will result in a better decision? How much diversity is enough?
2. The meeting participants were the same people from the same institution who analyzed a situation similar to one they had managed in the past. Predictably, there was little diversity of opinion because of the common experience. How could more diverse opinions/perspectives have been introduced by those with weaker ties to the situation?

References:

Araujo, E. B., Araujo, N. A. M., Moreira, A. A. Herrmann, H. J., and Andrade, J. S. Jr. (2017). Gender differences in scientific collaborations: Women are more egalitarian than men. *PLOS ONE* 12 (5): e0176791.

Chamorro-Premuzic, T. (2019). As long as we associate leadership with masculinity, women will be overlooked. *Harvard Business Review*, March 8.

Eagly, A., and Carli, L. L. (2007). Women and the labyrinth of leadership. *Harvard Business Review* 85 (9): 63–71.

Files, J. A. (2017). Speaker introduction at internal medicine grand rounds: Forms of address reveal gende bias. *Journal of Women's Health* 26 (5): 413–419.

Goldman, B. (2017). Two minds: The cognitive differences between men and women. *Stanford Medicine*, Spring, www.stanmed.stanford.edu.

Heim, P. (2005). *Hardball for Women: Winning at the Game of Business.* London: Plume.

Jena, A. B. (2016). Sex differences in physician salary in US public medical schools. *JAMA Internal Medicine* 176 (9):1294–1304.

Johnson, P. A., Widnall, S. E., and Benya, F. F., eds. (2018). Sexual harassment of women: Climate, culture and consequences in academic sciences, engineering and medicine. *The National Academies of Science, Engineering and Medicine Consensus Study Report.* Washington, DC: The National Academies Press.

Kay, K., and Shipman, C. (2014). *The Confidence Code: The Science and Art of Self-Assurance: What Women Should Know.* New York: Harper Business.

Rabinowitz, L. (2018). Recognizing blind spots – a remedy for gender bias in medicine. *New England Journal of Medicine* 378 (24): 2253–2255.

Rosener, J. (1995). *America's Competitive Secret: Women Managers.* New York: Oxford University Press.

Saujani, R. (2018). Founder/CEO, "Girls Who Code," speaking at TED talk.

Stone, L. With the best will in the world: How benevolent sexism shapes medical careers. https://orcid.org/0000-0001-8913-4117.

Wehner, M., Nead, K. T., Linos, K., and Linos, E. (2015). Plenty of moustaches but not enough women: Cross sectional study of medical leaders. *British Medical Journal*, December 16: 351.

Chapter FIFTEEN
The Big Picture in Summary

This physician roadmap is written to fill a gap. It touches on the 11 very basic points every physician leader must master. Achieving mastery of these points isn't the end, it's just the beginning. As I said at the start of this book, I have seen physicians make so many mistakes in meetings and in leadership situations. I was taken aback when, as president of the American Osteopathic Association, I was at a meeting in Washington, DC, and the president of a national organization of another health care profession introduced herself. In the course of the conversation she said, "My PhD is in leadership, what is yours in?" Oh! Yes, a bit snarky, but her point was that physicians weren't going to continue to be seen as leaders just because we think we should be.

This is a serious situation. As physicians, we are not always seen as leaders, and we are seldom trained to be leaders. This is not a good combination for today's times and situations. Physicians comprise only one of the professions that advocates for patients and good health care, but we are still a critical and strong voice for that ultimate goal. In this changing health care delivery and structure environment, our strong and effective voice is critically important. We simply can't afford to abdicate our responsibility to engage in the process—and we can't successfully engage in the process if we don't learn some leadership basics. Hence this roadmap.

There are many more things the physician leader needs to learn. The focus of this roadmap is on 11 things you simply must nail down as you move to the next set of knowledge and skills. Skipping these basic points on this road has led many well-intentioned physician leaders down a rocky, pothole-filled back road when the freeway express lane was nearby if they had just consulted this roadmap.

This is a very personal book with my stories, my examples, and referencing books and articles I have read. There are many more resources available and more are being written and published. As I said earlier, no article or book, including this one, can give you all the answers. It gives you ideas but it can't make you think. And while my experience is extensive, it is not exhaustive. (Sometimes it is exhausting!) Each situation you face may have nuances that mandate a different approach. This roadmap has been created to teach common issues and well-regarded approaches for a quick reference. Now go change the world! The world needs us!

General Resources

Daft, R. (2015). *The Leadership Experience* (6th Ed.). Stamford, CT: Cengage Learning.

Dalio, R. (2017). *Principles: Life and Work*. New York: Simon and Schuster.

Scisco, P., Biech, E., and Hallenbeck, G. (2017). *Compass: Your Guide for Leadership Development and Coaching*. Greensboro, NC: Center for Creative Leadership.

Watkins, M. (2013). *The First 90 Days: Proven Strategies for Getting up to Speed Faster and Smarter, Updated and Expanded*. Boston: Harvard Business School Publishing.

Acknowledgments

I have many people to acknowledge and thank for teaching me about leadership and thus bringing this book to press. I actually take on this task with some trepidation as I am sure I will inadvertently omit individuals who have also played equally pivotal roles in my career, but here goes. And I apologize in advance to those whom I have not included.

I have had two formal coaches, about whom I have written in this book. Mary Herrmann is currently the managing director for executive coaching at BPI Group. She gently helped guide me to first truly understand that I needed a coach and then she taught me so much about process. Carol Aschenbrener, MD, was the chief medical education officer at the Association of American Medical Colleges at the time and was my content coach, having been a provost and dean among her many roles in her career. Their formal teaching was invaluable in developing my leadership skills.

At the time, I did not recognize the importance of the role of sponsor as now described in this book, however I had two of the best, Frank Metzger, DO, and Bill Zipperer Jr., DO. We were residency mates, and then partnered in medical practice. Frank introduced me and both of them supported me in what was then a very rare role, a woman in consultative medical practice.

I have had many valuable mentors in leadership and in life. Two who are no longer with us were early guides and mentors, Mary Lou Butterworth, DO and Mary Burnett, DO. They were among the first women DOs I ever met, and they warmly guided me in my early career. Residency was the perfect opportunity to watch, work, and learn from the best, Ken Calabrese, DO, David Hitzeman, DO, and Dan Fieker, DO, all excellent physicians and leaders and who have continued to be colleagues and friends. Two pastors have modeled exemplary leadership and have mentored me, Roy Lawson, PhD, and the Reverend Dr. Dan Meyer, also lifelong friends. I will likewise always be indebted to the president and CEO of Midwestern University (MWU), Kathleen H. Goeppinger, PhD, who has also played a major role in my leadership life, first by hiring me as Dean of Chicago College of Osteopathic Medicine, then when I was working to learn how to be a dean, hiring Mary Herrmann as my coach on process. So many lessons from all these mentors are sprinkled throughout this book.

Speaking of my academic career, I would have never been successful without the mentoring of three other deans at MWU, who just happened to be women, Teresa Dombrowski Niiro, PhD, Nancy Fjortoft, PhD, and Jackie Smith, PhD. They taught me how to be a dean and a leader by guiding me and showing me how they led their respective colleges/student services so successfully. Add to this list my longtime friend Lori Kemper, DO, who later became an MWU dean and who also did and does mentor me still. More leadership lessons from them are incorporated into this book!

In putting together a book like this, I have benefited from wise counsel from friends and colleagues. I want to give a particular shout out for the detailed review by Clint Adams, DO, Natasha Bray, DO, Christian Cable, MD, Thomas Ely, DO, Robert Juhasz, DO, Edith Mitchell, MD, and Amanda Xi, MD. Invaluable assistance came from my long-time friend and colleague, BB Hill, who is master's-prepared in organization, training, and development. The book is so much better and clearer for their input.

I have another group for whom I am very grateful; our great Wiley team! Deborah Schindlar, Shannon Vargo and Sally Baker are as good as they come. They are so helpful and easy to work with. They truly understand what I'm striving to accomplish and I could not have asked for a better team to bring this book to fruition!

An acknowledgment statement would not be complete without including my family, which I am grateful for every day. Our parents, John and Willodean Hoesel, raised us to be all we can be, supporting whatever endeavor we chose, mine being a physician and leader. They modeled integrity and commitment to the goal. They demonstrated that grace and kindness comprise the proper approach to employ at all times and thus is required to become an effective leader. Sisters Sue Thurston, Nancy Martin, and Terry

Hanenburg are as good as any sisters can ever be. They are not only sisters but friends, again modeling those attributes taught by our parents.

All these people and so many more have been integral to the leadership lessons described in this book. At every step of my path, I have been able to reflect on their guidance and benefit from these wonderful role models. My goal, through this book, is to pay it forward.

About the Author

Karen J. Nichols, DO, MA, MACOI, FACP, CS-F is most recently the dean of the Midwestern University/Chicago College of Osteopathic Medicine (MWU/CCOM), serving from 2002 to July 2018. She took a leave to serve as president of the American Osteopathic Association (AOA) in 2010–2011. Prior to serving as dean, she was assistant dean, Post-Doctoral Education, and chair, Internal Medicine, at the MWU/Arizona College of Osteopathic Medicine since 1997. She was in the private practice of internal medicine and geriatrics in Mesa, Arizona, from 1985 through 2002. A graduate of the Kansas City University College of Osteopathic Medicine (KCU-COM) with a DO degree, she holds a master's degree in management with a specialty in healthcare administration from Central Michigan University.

In 2015, Dr. Nichols was selected for the highest honor given by the AOA, the Distinguished Service Award, as well as receiving a Presidential Citation in 2018. In 2015, she received the Robert A. Kistner DO Award, and then in 2020, received the Dale Dodson DO Award, the two highest honors bestowed by the American Association of Colleges of Osteopathic Medicine. Dr. Nichols received the 2014 Lifetime Achievement Award from the Arizona Osteopathic Medical Association (AOMA). She has received three Physician of the Year awards, from AOMA and Illinois Osteopathic Medical Society (IOMS) (twice) and presented the J.O. Watson named Lectureship to the Ohio Osteopathic Association (twice). She was the 2012 recipient of the KCU-COM Alumna of the Year award. She has received Distinguished Service Awards from the IOMS, and the alumni associations of CCOM and KCU-COM. Dr. Nichols holds eight honorary degrees.

She has served as president of the AOA, president of the AOMA, and president of the American College of Osteopathic Internists and was the first woman to hold all those positions. She is past president of the Institute of Medicine of Chicago Board of Governors.

In 2004, Dr. Nichols created the endowed Costin Institute for Osteopathic Medical Educators, sited at MWU/CCOM, a one-year hybrid fellowship that has graduated over 300 medical educators. Dr. Nichols teaches nationally and internationally on the topics of end-of-life care, physician leadership, and women leaders in medicine.

Index